INTRODUCTION TO EFFECTIVE MUSIC TEACHING

INTRODUCTION TO EFFECTIVE MUSIC TEACHING

Artistry and Attitude

Alfred S. Townsend

ROWMAN & LITTLEFIELD PUBLISHERS, INC.
Lanham • Boulder • New York • Toronto • Plymouth, UK

Published by Rowman & Littlefield Publishers, Inc.
A wholly owned subsidiary of
The Rowman & Littlefield Publishing Group, Inc.
4501 Forbes Boulevard, Suite 200, Lanham, Maryland 20706
http://www.rowmanlittlefield.com

Estover Road, Plymouth PL6 7PY, United Kingdom

British Library Cataloguing in Publication Information Available

Library of Congress Cataloging-in-Publication Data

Townsend, Alfred S.
  Introduction to effective music teaching : artistry and attitude / Alfred S.
Townsend.
       p. cm.
  Includes bibliographical references and index.
  ISBN 978-1-4422-0945-9 (cloth : alk. paper) — ISBN 978-1-4422-0946-6 (pbk. :
alk. paper) — ISBN 978-1-4422-0947-3 (electronic)
  1. Music—Instruction and study. I. Title.
  MT1.T77 2011
  780.71—dc22   2011014759

Printed in the United States of America

To Bette-Jeanne

Contents

Foreword

Alfred S. Townsend has produced a textbook that emphasizes the relationship between artistry and attitude as the most important ingredients for the success of a music teacher. The why, how, and what are examined as they relate to characteristics of a successful music teacher. His book is based on over forty years of successful music teaching at the elementary through university levels. The target audience is undergraduate music education majors, but his comments are not restricted to them. Included is a section on professional growth, appropriate for new as well as experienced teachers in a rapidly changing world.

Roger P. Phelps, Ph.D., professor emeritus, New York University

Acknowledgments

Many thanks go to my wife, Bette-Jeanne, and my sister, Elaine Blaser, for helpful suggestions and proofreading skills; and to my daughter, Jennifer, for offering advice in her field—early childhood, elementary, and special education.

I gratefully acknowledge Old Dominion University music professor Nancy Klein for her contribution to the leadership chapter. Thanks go to public school music educators and administrators Frank Garcia, Ashley Phillips, Steven Schopp, and James Cassara for their case study contributions in effective teaching and leadership. I am indebted to Old Dominion University librarian Elizabeth Hogue for her help; to public school chorus teacher Linda Boles, whose students contributed thoughts about music; to elementary music teacher Fernanda Veloso, who field tested ideas from this book; to James Scannell, Baldwin schools, for assistance; to Old Dominion University students Jonathan Duggan and Erika Mullen for converting my drawings into diagrams of effective teaching; and to Sara Jordan, Keith Smith, and Alyssa Montchal for contributing their philosophies of music education.

This book could not have been written without the enduring examples of effective artistry and attitude exhibited by the public school faculties with whom I have served as fellow teacher and administrator. In addition, I have drawn inspiration from the thousands of public school and university students I have taught over the years.

I especially applaud my editor, Patti Belcher, at Rowman & Littlefield, for her expert advice, calm in the face of craziness, keen eye, and the uncanny ability to juggle multiple tasks—all done with alacrity and élan. I am grateful to Chris Armstrong, elementary vocal and general music educator, Howard County Public Schools, for reviewing the manuscript and providing positive, constructive comments.

I am grateful to Roger Phelps, who wrote the foreword for this book. As coordinator of doctoral studies in music education, and chairman of the Department of Music and the Performing Arts at New York University, he also served on my Ph.D. committee. Despite his heavy workload, he always found the time to review in detail and offer direction for my dissertation. He also provided an inspiring example of effective music teaching in the doctoral courses I took from him. His distinguished career stands as a model for the effective combination of teaching artistry and attitude.

Above all, I thank Bette-Jeanne Townsend, my wife, who throughout her stellar music teaching career effectively combined artistry, attitude, faith, and learning. As a godly woman and an outstanding performer and teacher, she has inspired me beyond measure.

For years I have asked others about that one special teacher who profoundly influenced their life and learning. No one has ever asked me who that teacher was in my life. That person would be my mother, who also was my kindergarten teacher: Ruth Kathleen Townsend, MLS. Her scholarship, servant leadership, life priorities, and sterling character traits have left an indelible imprint on my life. God, family, books, and learning were the hallmarks of this remarkable woman. Soli Deo Gratias!

Introduction

What is an effective music teacher? I challenge anyone to come up with a formula that can be used to answer that question definitively. We cannot just feed numbers into an equation and produce a model for the effective music teacher, because in the field of education we are dealing with humans, not auto parts. Students and teachers possess infinite combinations of continually changing knowledge, backgrounds, personalities, and abilities. To try to quantify the confluence of these factors would be futile.

However, there are qualities of effective music teachers that have emerged over years of research from which we can learn and grow professionally. Given the complexity of the teaching and learning process, these qualities or traits of effective music teachers can be distilled into remarkably few groups. These groups reflect a productive combination of artistry and attitude, and align with six components of effective music teaching that will be explored later in the book.

As you read through the chapters you will review the historical context of music education in the United States and what the research literature has revealed about effective music teaching over the decades. You will also see how components of artistry and attitude combine in designing lesson plans and in the delivery of instruction.

In one chapter you will examine examples of effective communication that connect families with learning by involving parents in studying content along with their children. In other chapters you will explore the role of leadership in effective teaching and read what students have to say about effective teachers in their lives. You will then use all of this information in a process that will help you develop a personal philosophy of music education—what you believe is most important in teaching and learning. Using the material from this book you should be able to assess your own potential for effectiveness, grow professionally, and lead your students to more meaningful learning. After reading and reflecting on the ideas of the chapters that follow, I hope that you will become a more effective music teacher.

Throughout the book it will be apparent that effective teaching depends on a happy marriage between artistry and attitude. First, let's take a look at the area of artistry. What is it? And how will it fit into your development as an effective music teacher?

Artistry

In considering the concept of artistry, you might think in terms of performance areas such as musicality, expression, feeling, or personal interpretation, but there is also an artistry of teaching. Teaching, after all, can also be considered a performing art. The artistry of effective teaching is based on several areas that will be examined throughout the book. You will be challenged to build your artistry on a firm foundation of content command and mastery of methods. However, all of the content and methods knowledge in the world does not necessarily mean that your students will learn, or learn how to learn. Artistry in teaching contains layers of instruction and learning that work together to produce meaningful and productive interaction between teacher and student. But this interaction can have meaning only if your students can demonstrate understanding. To bring them to this understanding we depend on the critically important element of the "how" of effective teaching. This critical element is teacher attitude.

Attitude

In thinking about attitude you might come up with a vision of a special person who had a powerful influence on your life and learning—a parent, teacher, coach, pastor, priest, or rabbi. It was most likely *how* this special person said or taught something rather than *what* he or she said that made the "what" connect with you in a lasting way. This person had a gift at communicating content in a way that resonated with you at a particular time in your development. What can we learn from these especially effective teachers? Later you will read examples of these types of teachers, review their qualities, and reflect on how they caused all types of students to learn. To be a truly effective music teacher, artistry and attitude must work together. It takes command of content along with the ability to communicate that content in very special and often different ways to each student.

What is an effective music teacher? Certainly one answer is that the effective music teacher possesses mastery of content, knowledge, and methods together with attributes of attitude that cause students of all abilities and backgrounds to realize their full potential and succeed beyond even their own expectations. However, the proof of effective music teaching lies with the students.

What is an effective music teacher? Look to your students. Students are the real proof of effective teaching because if they are regularly present in your classroom or rehearsal space, and are trying to learn and still not learning, have you taught them? Look to your students to assess your effectiveness as a teacher. So, even though there is no magic formula to precisely produce the effective music teacher, the effective teacher can be described as one whose students realize their potential, learn how to learn, and develop creative competency and a sustaining intellectual and artistic curiosity.

In the chapters that follow, you will find signposts to guide you as you seek the most productive path to effective music teaching. To start your journey, take a moment right now to list (1) three to five reasons why you believe it is important and necessary for all students to study music, (2) three to five traits that music teachers should possess to be the most effective in causing students to learn, and (3) four to six things that you believe are most important for your students to learn as a result of your teaching. Then write one paragraph that demonstrates how you intend to help your students learn those four to six things. Keep your responses in mind as you go through the book. As you approach its conclusion, you will be asked to review what you have written and discuss to what degree, if any, your ideas about teaching and learning have changed. This process will be helpful as you write a personal philosophy of music education that delineates your beliefs about teaching and learning music.

The first chapter sets effective teaching within a historical context and provides a review of what research has revealed about traits of the effective music teacher.

1

The Historical and Research Context of Effective Music Teaching

Historical Context of Effective Music Teaching

On August 24, 1830, in Boston at the Representatives Hall, William Channing Woodbridge delivered a speech to the American Institute of Instruction titled "On Vocal Music as a Branch of Common Education." As part of the event, a local church musician and choirmaster, Lowell Mason, arranged to have a group of boys demonstrate by their singing how much they had learned by studying music. They sang three songs: "The Morning Call," "The Garden," and "The Rising Sun."[1] Lowell Mason's association with Woodbridge began at that event,[2] which served as a harbinger for the study of music as a subject in the public schools.

William Channing Woodbridge (1794–1845) was a published scholar of geography and a minister who was enthusiastic about education in the United States, particularly music and learning. Lowell Mason (1792–1872), often referred to as the father of music education in the United States, was an accomplished singer and played several instruments. He performed as a soloist and led church choirs in Massachusetts and Savannah, Georgia, and became quite well known as a composer, music teacher, and music publisher. In 1833, he, along with Woodbridge and other businessmen, founded the private Boston Academy of Music. Mason taught at the school and was one of its leaders.

Johann Heinrich Pestalozzi and Lowell Mason

Woodbridge and Mason embraced the theories and principles of Swiss educator Johann Heinrich Pestalozzi (1746–1827). "Pestalozzi rejected the school

4

practices of memorization and recitation that were then common, and substituted for them observation, experimentation, and reasoning. He was the first to attempt to link the educational process to the natural development of the child."[3]

During a trip to Europe (1824–1829), Woodbridge observed Hans Georg Nägeli, a disciple of Pestalozzi, employing Pestalozzi's principles in his instruction. These principles, modified for music instruction, were as follows[4]:

1. To teach sounds before signs—to make the child sing before he learns written notes or their names.
2. To lead the child to observe, by hearing and imitating sounds, their resemblances and differences, their agreeable and disagreeable effects, rather than explaining these things to him. By this principle, the child was to be an active, rather than passive, learner.
3. To teach but one thing at a time—rhythm, melody, and expression are taught and practiced separately before the child is called to the difficult task of attending to all at once.
4. To make children practice each step of each of these divisions until they master it before passing to the next.
5. To give the principles and theory after practice, and as an induction from it.
6. To analyze and practice the elements of articulate sound in order to apply them to music.
7. To have the names of the notes correspond to those used in instrumental music.[5]

Mason incorporated these and other principles into his *Manual of the Boston Academy of Music, for Instruction in the Elements of Vocal Singing on the System of Pestalozzi*. From this manual and a series of subsequent writings, Mason's philosophy founded on Pestalozzian thought and practice has been summarized as follows:

1. The purpose of music in the schools is to create musically intelligent adults rather than to train professional musicians.
2. The quality of music used in teaching is of vital importance. Only music of artistic value should be used in the music class.
3. The process used in teaching is of greater importance and more lasting value than the product of that teaching.
4. To be most effective, music education must begin with the young child.
5. Music is a discipline involving all the senses and contributing to the total development of the human being.
6. To achieve in music, work is necessary.
7. Practical experience must come before theory; and theory must grow out of that practical experience.
8. Musical literacy is both a possible and desirable goal for most people.[6]

Lowell Mason and the Birth of Music Education

Mason believed strongly that the study of music edified the citizenry and increased happiness. He was determined to bring music into the public schools. So during the 1837–1838 school year, Mason taught vocal music in one Boston public school without pay, and had his students perform publicly to much acclaim. At the end of the academic year, Boston's mayor requested a report on the music instruction from the school:

> The reply praised the effect of music on the students and the quality of Mason's instruction in the *Boston Music Gazette* on July 25, 1838: "Many who at the outset of the experiment believed they had neither ear or voice, now sing with confidence and considerable accuracy; and others who could hardly tell one sound from another, now sing the scale with ease; sufficiently proving that the musical susceptibility is in a good degree improvable."[7]

Mason was such an effective teacher that

> on August 28, 1838, the Boston School Committee instructed the Committee on Music to appoint a teacher [Mason] of vocal music in the public schools of Boston. By this action, music was approved for what may have been the first time in the United States as a subject of the public school curriculum, like English and mathematics, to be supported with school funds. Music had been taught in schools before, but never as an integral subject of the curriculum.[8]

The Growth of Music Education

During the sixty years or so that followed Mason's groundbreaking appointment, music as a distinct subject grew in favor and became part of the curriculum of many public schools across the country. Secondary education, in particular, grew steadily during the first part of the twentieth century, and with it interest in providing music as part of the regular curriculum. Included in this growth was the introduction of school orchestras and bands. The increasing popularity of these groups was, in large part, due to the rise in the number and prominence of professional orchestras and military bands. Today, public school music programs include marching bands, jazz groups, mariachi bands, steel bands, and electronic music classes in addition to traditional bands, choruses, orchestras, and classroom music study. But along with the growth of public school music programs there has always been the need to convince parents, communities, and government agencies of the importance of music education programs in the public schools for all children, and the need for adequate funding to support such programs.

Teacher Training

With the introduction and expansion of public school music teaching came the need for specially trained teachers. From the time of Mason until the end of the nineteenth century, both public and private teacher-preparation institutions, called "normal schools," prepared students in the content and methods of instruction. At the beginning of the twentieth century, these normal schools evolved into teachers colleges with four-year baccalaureate programs. Today, teacher-preparation programs in a wide array of subjects proliferate in colleges and universities across the country.

Music Education and Change

Since the time of Pestalozzi and Lowell Mason, ideas about the role of music in the schools and methods of instruction in general have been in flux. Teacher-centered learning of the 1800s and before featured specific content that was delivered to students using memorization and recitation as essential components of instruction. Pestalozzi's principles challenged this approach and foreshadowed the philosophy of John Dewey in the early twentieth century. Dewey's philosophy of educating the whole child naturally included the arts; however, education changed in the United States when in 1957 the Soviet Union successfully launched the satellite Sputnik. This event highlighted the inadequacies of technology in the United States. In response, school programs concentrated funding and curriculum emphasis on the sciences. However, even though the sciences received primary attention, some support for arts development eventually was provided via federal funding for the Yale Seminar of 1963. Participants at the seminar examined public school music education and, among other concerns, were critical of the quality of the music literature used for study in the nation's schools.

To affirm the importance and role of music education in the public schools, and counter the criticisms of the Yale Seminar, which included few music educators as participants, the Music Educators National Conference (MENC; now MENC: The National Association for Music Education) president Louis Wersen and former president Robert Choate formed the Tanglewood Symposium. Participants at the symposium were made up of a wide range of music and nonmusic educators, professional musicians, corporate and government representatives, scientists, and sociologists, among others.

The Tanglewood Symposium

The Tanglewood Symposium was held in 1967 at the Berkshire Center in Massachusetts and was sponsored by MENC together with Boston University and the Theodore Presser Foundation. The symposium theme,

"Music in American Society," was reflected in the ensuing Tanglewood Declaration, which states,

> We believe that education must have as major goals the art of living, the building of personal identity, and nurturing creativity. Since the study of music can contribute much to these ends, *we now call for music to be placed in the core of the school curriculum.*
>
> The arts afford a continuity with the aesthetic tradition in man's history. Music and other fine arts, largely nonverbal in nature, reach close to the social, psychological, and physiological roots of man in his search for identity and self-realization.
>
> Educators must accept the responsibility for developing opportunities which meet man's individual needs and the needs of a society plagued by the consequences of changing values, alienation, hostility between generations, racial and international tensions, and the challenges of a new leisure. [italics in original]

Music educators at Tanglewood agreed that

1. Music serves best when its integrity as an art is maintained.
2. Music of all periods, styles, forms, and cultures belongs in the curriculum. The musical repertory should be expanded to involve music of our time in its rich variety, including currently popular teen age music and avant-garde music, American folk music, and the music of other cultures.
3. Schools and colleges should provide adequate time for music in programs ranging from preschool through adult or continuing education.
4. Instruction in the arts should be a general and important part of education in the senior high school.
5. Developments in educational technology, educational television, programmed instruction, and computer-assisted instruction should be applied to music study and research.
6. Greater emphasis should be placed on helping the individual student fulfill his needs, goals, and potentials.
7. The music education profession must contribute its skills, proficiencies, and insights toward assisting in the solution of urgent social problems as in the "inner city" or other areas with culturally deprived individuals.
8. Programs of teacher education must be expanded and improved to provide music teachers who are specially equipped to teach high school courses in the history and literature of music, courses in the humanities and related arts, and music teachers equipped to work with the very young, with adults, with the disadvantaged, and with the emotionally disturbed.[9]

The National Standards for Music Education

In spite of the statements that came out of the 1967 Tanglewood Symposium, and the specific call for music to be placed in the core of the school curriculum, public school music programs across the nation still lacked comprehensive standards and depended on uneven local support for status in the curriculum. It took years to develop national music education coherence.

The stimulus for national music education reform came from a 1983 government commission that detailed devastating shortcomings of the entire U.S. educational system in the document "A Nation at Risk." This report sent shock waves throughout the country. In response, the federal government and other agencies called for subject area standards to be formed. MENC and other arts organizations received funding to develop such standards. Starting in 1992, MENC, together with representatives from other arts groups, developed the National Standards for Arts Education, which were published in 1994. The document contained national standards for music, the visual arts, theatre, and dance in grades K–12. Also in 1994, the Goals 2000: Educate America Act was signed into law. This act included the development of national standards in education and specifically included the arts for the first time as one of the core academic subjects. The 1994 National Standards for Music Education developed by MENC detail what every student should know and be able to do as a result of school music study.

The nine MENC National Standards for Music Education are as follows:

1. Singing, alone and with others, a varied repertoire of music
2. Performing on instruments, alone and with others, a varied repertoire of music
3. Improvising melodies, variations, and accompaniments
4. Composing and arranging music within specified guidelines
5. Reading and notating music
6. Listening to, analyzing, and describing music
7. Evaluating music and music performances
8. Understanding relationships between music, the other arts, and disciplines outside the arts
9. Understanding music in relation to history and culture[10]

MENC also developed Performance Standards broken down by grade level that align with each of the nine National Standards and are available on MENC's website at www.menc.org in two online publications: *The National Music Education Standards (The School Music Program: A New Vision)* and *Performance Standards for Music: Strategies and Benchmarks for Assessing Progress Toward the National Standards, Grades PreK–12.*

A summary statement from the 1994 National Standards for Arts Education provides a compelling need for such comprehensive standards and their implementation.

The educational success of our children depends on creating a society that is both literate and imaginative, both competent and creative. That goal depends, in turn, on providing children with tools not only for understanding that world but for contributing to it and making their own way. Without the arts to help shape students' perceptions and imaginations, our children stand every chance of growing into adulthood as culturally disabled. We must not allow that to happen.

Without question, the Standards presented here will need supporters and allies to improve how arts education is organized and delivered. They have the potential to change education policy at all levels, and to make a transforming impact across the entire spectrum of education.

Teachers, of course, will be the leaders in this process. In many places, more teachers with credentials in the arts, as well as better-trained teachers in general, will be needed. Site-based management teams, school boards, state education agencies, state and local arts agencies, and teacher education institutions will all have a part to play, as will local mentors, artists, local arts organizations, and members of the community. Their support is crucial for the Standards to succeed. But the primary issue is the ability to bring together and deliver a broad range of competent instruction. All else is secondary.

In the end, truly successful implementation can come about only when students and their learning are at the center, which means motivating and enabling them to meet the Standards. With a steady gaze on that target, these Standards can empower America's schools to make changes consistent with the best any of us can envision, for our children and for our society.[11]

In 2007, an MENC task force reviewed the 1994 National Standards and among other findings reported that all fifty states use the National Standards, model their standards on the National Standards, or have standards that are entirely consistent with the National Standards. The 2007 review also revealed that there seemed to be a need for replacing or revising the accompanying Achievement Standards for each grade level in the general music program through grade 8, and for each elective course offering in the secondary schools. A task force has recommended a further review of the 1994 Achievement Standards that align with the nine National Standards. Further information about the standards and the work of the 2007 task force is available on the MENC website at www.menc.org.

The MENC Standards and Music Education Today

From the inception of public school music programs in 1838 to the present we can see the persistent challenge of keeping music education alive and growing in the public schools. Along with this challenge we must adapt our programs and teaching approaches to meet the needs of a changing world and student population. We now have national and state standards for learning in music that have proven effective in helping us maintain parity with other core subjects and provide clearly articulated goals for learning by all students. These standards also provide teachers, students, parents, and administrators with benchmarks for assessment so progress can be noted and rewarded. With the defined Performance Standards that accompany the National Standards and some state standards, sequential units of study and lesson plans can be more easily and effectively designed to help students succeed. But standards and lesson plans are not enough. Students await the leadership of the effective music teacher, the most powerful and important component of the learning process. What does the research literature reveal about music teaching effectiveness?

The Research Context of Effective Music Teaching

Against the backdrop of music education history, it will be helpful to trace the results of effective music teaching research over the decades. The quest to find what traits quality teachers possess has a long history. As far back as 1896, H. E. Kratz sought the characteristics of the best teachers by eliciting the views of school children.[12] Long before that time, in a very practical way, the Boston city fathers tested the quality of Lowell Mason's instruction. Mason had to demonstrate the effectiveness of his teaching for a full year before he was formally hired and paid. His effectiveness was determined by the quality of his students' public performances. Does that sound familiar?

Currently, our music programs are very much evaluated formally and informally on the quality of our ensemble performances, but at the core of effective teaching is the *progress* of individual students whether in the classroom or on the stage. The effective music teacher is the one who is able to meet students where they are and enable them to realize their full potential, and perhaps move beyond even their own expectations.

Traits of the Effective Music Teacher

What are the traits of such a teacher? Over a broad span of many decades, the research literature has repeatedly shown that the traits of the effective music teacher are quite similar in reflecting a combination of artistry and attitude. As you go through the traits of the effective music teacher contained in the following research overview, think about how you will apply them to your day-to-day contact with students.

Research: Pre-1990

A review of research from the 1980s and before is contained in the article "Teacher Effectiveness Research: A Review and Comparison."[13] In this article the authors refer to several descriptive studies from the 1980s. One study reviewed provides a synthesis of music teacher effectiveness research and practical findings.

That synthesis reports that an effective music teacher embodies the following traits:

- is enthusiastic
- possesses a warm personality
- takes a personal interest in students
- presents material in a clear manner
- teaches at a brisk pace
- plans a variety of activities within the class period
- balances praise and criticism
- has a desire to improve
- uses discipline techniques focused on communication of expectations[14]

From a review of other studies from the 1980s, the authors conclude that more traits of an effective music teacher include the following:

- is adept at human relationships
- is an independent thinker
- possesses a strong need to accomplish tasks
- has a creative teaching style
- is able to adapt instruction to student needs
- maintains an appropriate rehearsal atmosphere
- balances rehearsal and teacher talk effectively
- is thoroughly prepared for class
- uses high-quality literature[15]

Research: 1990s

In 1997, David J. Teachout examined elements for successful music teaching in *Preservice and Experienced Teachers' Opinions of Skills and Behaviors Important to Successful Music Teaching*. Preservice and experienced teachers were asked to rate forty teacher skills and behaviors relative to their importance to successful music teaching in the first three years of experience.[16]

Seven behaviors and skills out of the ten top-ranked items were common to both preservice and experienced music teachers: (1) be mature and have self-control, (2) be able to motivate students, (3) possess strong leadership skills, (4) involve students in the learning process, (5) display confidence, (6) be organized, and (7) employ a positive approach. It is instructive to make note of these seven items that both experienced and preservice teachers identified as important skills and behaviors.[17] Consider these items that have support from the research as you work to develop your own effective teaching approaches.

Beyond the seven behaviors and skills common to both experienced and preservice teachers, other skills and behaviors ranked by experienced and preservice music teachers showed a difference of viewpoints.[18] For ease of comparison, I have placed the rankings in table 1.1. Compare these rankings and you will notice that once you become a teacher, your ideas of what is important in interacting with students might change.

Table 1.1.   Music Teacher Skills and Behavior Chart

Skills and Behaviors	Experienced Teachers' Ranking	Preservice Teachers' Ranking
Be enthusiastic, energetic	3	15
Maximize time on task	12	22
Maintain student behavior	1	14
Be patient	7	19
Be creative, imaginative, and spontaneous	30	19
Display a high level of musicianship	22	11

So we observe that out of forty teacher skills and behaviors, the experienced music teachers in the research study put the greatest emphasis on maintaining student behavior. This emphasis could be because these teachers have observed that effective teaching and learning is more likely to take place in an orderly environment. In addition, you can see from the chart that experienced music teachers are more likely to view enthusiasm and energy, patience, and time on task as important than preservice music teachers. Interestingly, the experienced music teachers who participated in the study viewed creativity, imagination, spontaneity, and a high level of musicianship as less important than did the preservice music teachers.

These results provide a useful comparison of opinions from preservice and experienced teachers that will be helpful as you think about what skills and behaviors will be most important in your teaching. It is also important to note the seven skills and behaviors that are common to both the new and experienced music teachers. Each of these is linked to teacher attributes of attitude that we will examine later. These skills and behaviors will also figure prominently in the chapter on leadership, and in a discussion in later chapters about the six components of effective music teaching—content, communication, comprehension, dedication, structure, and character.

From these pre–twenty-first-century studies we already see a picture emerging of the effective music teacher as one whose teaching is driven by sterling qualities of attitude. This picture becomes quite clear as we review the information contained in the following later sources.

Research: 2000s

In his book, *Teaching Music in the Secondary Schools*, Charles R. Hoffer discusses the following important traits of the effective music teacher: (1) honest optimism, (2) establishing and encouraging an atmosphere of openness where students won't be afraid to make mistakes, (3) humor integrated with learning, (4) consistent responses, and (5) a pleasant, optimistic outlook.[19] Hoffer makes the point that by developing these traits, you will improve student-teacher relationships, create a positive, secure learning atmosphere, and instill confidence and pride of accomplishment in your students.

To prepare for the student-teaching experience, the following research is of particular value. The 2008 study *High School Instrumental Students' Perceptions of Effective Music Student Teacher Traits* by Steven N. Kelly[20] identifies skills and behaviors that certain high school students believe are most important for student teachers to possess.

Kelly surveyed high school band and orchestra students who were asked to rate student-teacher skills and behaviors "regarding the degree of importance with which each trait should be exhibited by a student teacher in a music class."[21] "The skills and behaviors receiving the highest mean scores were (1) is able to apply knowledge, (2) being competent, (3) has a positive behavior, (4) is respectful of students, (5) provides clear verbal instructions, and (6) displays confidence as a teacher."[22] The findings reflect the work of other researchers that found effective teaching is frequently influenced by skills and behaviors not requiring direct use of music knowledge or skills. Responding participants indicated that music student teachers should consider displaying a variety of personal characteristics and instructional behaviors, such as a teacher's positive personality, confidence, and presentation style.[23] This view of teaching from the high school student perspective demonstrates the need for you to develop effective strategies for the delivery of instruction together with heightened qualities of character and attitude.

Recent Narrative Research

A 2009 article by Manny Brand in the *Australian Journal of Music Education* discusses current research in music teacher effectiveness.[24]

> Contemporary research in music teacher effectiveness employs a broad range of methodologies and improved research techniques including use of larger sample sizes to permit more meaningful statistical analyses, and formulation and use of more sophisticated classroom observation and

coding instruments. Additionally, using narrative descriptions of effective music teachers, a number of studies now attempt to account for and emphasize context and focus on the individual teacher and class as the unit of analysis.[25]

Brand continues by referring to his own narrative descriptive work from 2006 in which he studied and observed, in depth, fifteen music teachers from nine countries in Southeast Asia and China.[26] He found that effective music teachers possess a number of qualities such as musicianship, charisma, personality, style, flexibility, tolerance, sincerity, responsiveness, and an underlying ability to create a near-magical connection with children.[27] Brand reports that all of the music teachers he observed exhibited the following traits: (1) they were extremely knowledgeable about the aspects of music they taught, (2) they had high energy and enthusiasm, and (3) they made a huge investment in time that it takes for successful teaching in preparing, thinking, planning, studying, reviewing, making rehearsal notes, marking up scores, finding new songs and musical activities, and locating that perfect movement that will enhance the children's understanding of, for example, the phrasing.[28]

Brand also found that these effective music teachers in Asia were especially spontaneously resourceful and responsive in their teaching, and were especially effective in finding and utilizing "teachable moments" to preserve the freshness and excitement of their teaching. Other teaching qualities observed in these effective music teachers included (1) their students knowing their teacher's expectations regarding both musical performance and student behavior, to the extent that these music students were often able to exceed beyond their own expectations; (2) masterful communication skills showing that they genuinely cared for their students; and (3) serving as beacons of inspiration for their students.[29] Throughout the sources reviewed thus far, you can see that the qualities most often cited as important to effective music teaching reflect artistry (command of content and mastery of methods) combined with traits of positive teacher attitude.

Important Teaching Skills and Advice to New Teachers

Earlier you read one study that reported high school students' perceptions concerning important traits for student teachers, and in another study what preservice and experienced teachers thought were important qualities for effective teaching. A more recent study, *Surveying Colorado Band Directors' Opinions of Skills and Characteristics Important to Successful Music Teaching*,[30] was conducted by three music education faculty members from the University of Colorado. The study reinforces those findings and adds advice experienced teachers offer to first-year teachers. Even though this study is restricted to band directors, any music teacher will certainly benefit from the results. As part of the investigation, the researchers gathered band directors' opinions of skills and characteristics important to teaching. Survey respondents ranked lists of music teaching and personal skills or characteristics in order of importance and answered open-ended items regarding advice for first-year teachers and the struggles and rewards of band directing.

> The highest ranked of the 10 personal characteristics was "enthusiastic, energetic," suggesting that the participants perceived teacher affect to be a critical element of successful teaching. The highest-ranked teaching skills were "be able to motivate students" and "maintain excellent classroom management." . . . The highest-ranked music characteristics were "maintain high musical standards," "display a high level of musicianship," and "be knowledgeable of subject matter materials." . . . With the exception of "display a high level of musicianship," all of the aforementioned items were ranked in the top 15 out of a list of 40 skills and characteristics by both preservice and experienced teachers in Teachout's (1997) study [cited previously in note 16]. The item rankings from both studies suggest that demonstrating enthusiasm, being able to motivate and manage students, and maintaining high music standards are still some of the most valued characteristics of successful music teachers in the field. . . .
>
> The most commonly cited topics of advice the research participants had for first year teachers were: developing patience and a sense of perseverance in regard to long-term program development; forming relationships with colleagues, students, and parents; and being organized with respect to preparation and communication. . . .
>
> The reported struggles of being a band director reflect issues related to student motivation, classroom management, adequate funding, and dealing with administrators.[31]

As you continue on in this book, you will learn that these research findings will be supported by additional reports from front-line teachers and what you have experienced in your own schooling. Your teaching artistry combined with your attributes of attitude will inform the way you connect with students to affect their learning.

Summary

So we see that the search for effective music teachers started early (1837) with Lowell Mason's experiences, and has continued for decades with the study of what makes a music teacher effective. It continues because our world is changing and along with it our student population. Such study is a worthy effort because we need to adjust to this often tumultuous, ever-shrinking world—a world in which students and teachers face increasingly complex and conflicting family, social, religious, economic, and political issues that directly affect teaching and learning.

Reflect on the effective teaching research literature in this chapter, keeping in mind that it contains teaching traits that will be useful as you construct your philosophy of music education later in the book. From the research that spans the years, it is apparent the effective music teacher can be characterized by success in combining knowledge of content and methods with positive attitudinal traits to affect student growth. Even though the research literature demonstrates that there really is no magic formula that can be used to create an effective music teacher on demand, there are characteristics of effective teaching worthy of emulation that do appear repeatedly in those teachers who enjoy success with a wide range of students.

You have examined the historical context of effective teaching and reviewed the traits of effective teaching as revealed by research. Against this background, in the next chapter, a sharper profile of effective teaching emerges. You will see how the traits of effective teaching play out in the school setting, and you will explore how the effective music teacher combines content knowledge and methods of instruction in the area of teaching artistry.

For Reflection, Discussion, Assignment

1. For each of the nine MENC standards listed in this chapter, write one paragraph that demonstrates how you intend to implement each one in your teaching. Give examples of what activities or other experiences you might use with students to satisfy each of the nine standards. Be prepared to discuss your responses.

2. Using the information from this chapter, the following resources, or other sources, create a one-page timeline that shows the origins and development to the present day, for your anticipated area of specialty. For example, your area of specialty might be elementary or secondary classroom music, band, chorus, or orchestra. The timeline should contain the origin, five historical highlights, and the condition of your area today. For example, if you are intending to be an elementary classroom music teacher, identify the origin of classroom music followed by five important milestones that have led us up to where we are now. Use and document at least two sources to support the information for your timeline.

3. Study the characteristics of effective music teaching that appear in this chapter and choose eight to twelve of them that personally resonate with you and could be the most important characteristics

of your teaching. List the characteristics and explain why you chose each one. Discuss how each relates to the way you intend to teach. Give examples of how you might apply each characteristic to actual classroom or rehearsal situations.

4. Reflect on your own student experiences and identify what effective teacher characteristics you observed in at least three teachers you have had. Without naming the teacher or location, identify and discuss characteristics that your teachers demonstrated that tended to *hinder* your learning and how you would do things differently.

5. As in the previous question, identify and discuss characteristics exhibited by teachers that have been most effective in *helping* you to learn.

Resources

Abeles, Harold F., and Lori A. Custodero. *Critical Issues in Music Education: Contemporary Theory and Practice.* New York: Oxford University Press, 2010.

Abeles, Harold F., Charles R. Hoffer, and Robert H. Klotman. *Foundations of Music Education,* 2nd ed. Belmont, CA: Thomson Higher Education, 1995.

Brand, Manny. "Music Teacher Effectiveness: Selected Historical and Contemporary Research Approaches." *Australian Journal of Music Education* 1 (2009): 13–18.

Campbell, Patricia Shehan, and Carol Scott Kassner. *Music in Childhood,* 3rd ed. New York: Schirmer, 2009.

Choate, Robert A., ed. *Documentary Report of the Tanglewood Symposium.* Washington, DC: Music Educators National Conference, 1968.

Choate, Robert A., Charles B. Fowler, Charles E. Brown, and Louis G. Wersen. "The Tanglewood Symposium: Music in American Society." *Music Educators Journal* 54, no. 3 (1967): 49–80.

Choksy, Lois, Robert M. Abramson, Avon E. Gillespie, David Woods, and Frank York. *Teaching Music in the Twenty-First Century,* 2nd ed. Upper Saddle River, NJ: Prentice-Hall, 2001.

Cruickshank, Donald, Kim K. Metcalf, and Deborah Bainer Jenkins. *The Act of Teaching.* New York: McGraw Hill, 2008.

Grant, Joe W., and Lynn E. Drafall. "Teacher Effectiveness Research: A Review and Comparison." *Bulletin of the Council for Research in Music Education* 108 (Spring 1991): 31–48.

Hoffer, Charles, R. *Music for Elementary Classroom Teachers,* 2nd ed. Long Grove, IL: Waveland Press, 2004.

———. *Teaching Music in the Secondary Schools,* 5th ed. Belmont, CA: Wadsworth/Thomson Learning, 2001.

Kelly, Steven N. "High School Instrumental Students' Perceptions of Effective Music Student Teacher Traits." *Journal of Music Teacher Education* 17 (Spring 2008): 83–91.

Lautzenheiser, Tim. *The Art of Successful Teaching: A Blend of Content and Context.* Chicago: GIA, 1992.

Mark, Michael L., and Charles L. Gary. *A History of American Music Education.* Lanham, MD: Rowman & Littlefield Education, 2007.

Mason, Lowell. *Manual of the Boston Academy of Music, for Instruction in the Elements of Vocal Singing on the System of Pestalozzi.* Boston: Carter and Hendee, 1834.

MENC: The National Association for Music Education. *Performance Standards for Music: Strategies and Benchmarks for Assessing Progress Toward the National Standards, Grades PreK–12.* Reston, VA: MENC, 1996.

———. *The School Music Program: A New Vision.* Reston, VA: MENC, 1994.

———. "What Personal Characteristics Do I Need?" *Teacher to Teacher, A Music Educator's Survival Guide.* Reston, VA: MENC, 2001.

Miksza, Peter, Matthew Roeder, and Dana Biggs. "Surveying Colorado Band Directors' Opinions of Skills and Characteristics Important to Successful Music Teaching." *Journal of Research in Music Education* 57, no. 4 (January 2010): 364–81.

Pelton, Robert P. *Action Research for Teacher Candidates: Using Classroom Data to Enhance Instruction.* Lanham, MD: Rowman & Littlefield Education, 2010.

Teachout, David J. "Preservice and Experienced Teachers' Opinions of Skills and Behavior Important to Successful Music Teaching." *Journal of Research in Music Education* 45 (Spring 1997): 41–50.

2

Artistry in Effective Teaching: Command of Content and Mastery of Methods

Effective music teaching is artistry; however, artistry contains much more than just musicianship in performance. It goes far beyond the performer on the stage and extends to all aspects of music, including teaching and learning. Effective teaching itself is a performing art. Effective teaching is prepared performance. Teaching artistry envelopes command of content and mastery of methods all unlocked by the key of teacher attitude. The effective music teacher is successful in combining artistry and attitude, and applying the result to the needs of students possessing all backgrounds and abilities.

Artistry begins with the intimate knowledge of your subject and extends to the methods you will use to engage students in learning. We start with the area of content because everything that follows is based on what you know about your subject. Without this command of content, your teaching will be like trying to draw water from an empty well.

Command of Content

The area of content is complex as it is composed of all that you have learned in your college coursework and studied on your major instrument or voice. Effective music teachers are dedicated to developing their content knowledge in order to form a solid foundation for all instruction, and to provide a rich resource for leading students ever upward in learning.

Your content background from college study provides you with the theoretical and technical expertise to lead all types of students in the study of sequential concepts and skills. This sequence can come from a variety of sources. The school district in which you teach might have a syllabus of music that contains benchmarks of achievement for each grade preK–12.

Or the content and outcomes of the music curriculum could be contained in a graded textbook series or in graded performance literature. Sequential content study is also intertwined with methodologies developed by people such as Orff, Kodaly, Dalcroze, Gordon, and Suzuki. Whatever curriculum you will be following, the content should be aligned with state standards for learning, if they exist, and the National Standards for Music Education propagated by MENC: The National Association for Music Education, along with the companion MENC Performance Standards for Music. Access the National Standards and Performance Standards available at www.menc.org via Resources > Online Publications > *The National Music Education Standards (The School Music Program: A New Vision)* and *Performance Standards for Music.* You should become familiar with these resources as they provide foundational content components, clear benchmarks for sequential instruction, and examples of how the standards are assessed throughout all grade levels. After reviewing these publications, you will know what the expectations are for achievement in each of the nine standards so you will be better able to design activities and choose literature to meet them.

Whether you are an instrumental or vocal classroom teacher, the content of your lessons should be based on high-quality literature for soloists, performing ensembles, or for the music classroom. English and art teachers make sure they use the works of the best writers and artists as the basis of study.[1] I am sure that all music teachers want the same. With increasingly limited class time available, why waste this precious time and spend energy using works of questionable quality? Plus, if you use high-quality literature in all areas of the music program, it will strengthen your position among the other subjects and provide a compelling reason for music study in your school and district. Spending time to choose literature carefully ensures the maximization of tight budgets and the immediate effectiveness and lasting value of your purchase.

In the article "The Importance of High-Quality Literature," Diane Persellin uses the image of a garden to underscore the positive effect of such literature:

> A fine gardener knows the importance of using the best, high-quality seeds. He or she understands that unless these seeds are the best that can be found, no amount of fancy fertilizer, rain, sun, or diligent weeding will yield the best flower garden. The gardener will always be struggling to make up for the basic weakness of the inferior seeds that were planted.
>
> Of course, the gardener cannot rely only on fine seeds and then neglect the garden. It takes a combination of good seeds (fine repertoire) and careful nurturing (strong teaching) to result in a beautiful garden (a brilliant concert), but the importance of the excellent seeds cannot be underestimated.[2]

Whether choosing performance literature for your ensembles or selecting songs and other music for study in the classroom, you will be well on your way to cultivating an extraordinary "garden" if you use the finest "seeds" available.

However, as Persellin indicates, there is more to effective teaching and learning than just choosing high-quality literature. Consider the following story about two music teachers—one new to the profession, one a helpful veteran.

The Tale of Teacher A and Teacher B

Teacher A (TA) was a new elementary band teacher who was experiencing puzzling rehearsal problems. The students weren't playing up to their ability levels. At times they were talkative, restless, and unfocused. To make things worse, it seemed as if they weren't practicing at home. Rehearsals usually ended with a lecture to the students on why they must practice and why they must pay attention during rehearsals. TA would exclaim, "The concert is coming soon! We don't want to embarrass ourselves! Your family will be in the audience! You must watch me, listen to me and to each other, and above all practice at home!"

TA often left school angry, feeling defeated and frustrated. TA thought, "Why don't they play better? The only reason I chose this music was because I thought they would like it." TA lost sleep trying to think of ways to teach the music so the students would perform with skill and intelligence. The more TA tried to get the students to succeed, the more TA failed. TA's university methods professor had warned against rote teaching, but in desperation TA resorted to that method. The students did learn one piece that way but when the next piece was handed out, the students asked, "How does this piece go?" So TA had to teach in the same fashion. TA sang and clapped the rhythms for the students, and then had them imitate what they heard. At one point, TA even chanted the slide positions in rhythm to get the trombones to play the correct notes.

Thankfully, TA realized that the students were not being enabled to learn how to learn. TA knew that the students would not be able to transfer their learning to new situations. Once they moved on to the next teacher, they would have to find someone else to show them how each piece would "go."

TA couldn't imagine teaching this way for the next thirty or forty years, so TA contacted a veteran teacher, Teacher B (TB), from another building, whose bands consistently performed literature at a high level of execution and expression. TB's students seemed happy, learned more pieces than TA's students, and, to boot, TB's band could sight read pretty well. TB even engaged students in improvising over short chord progressions.

TA discussed the problem with TB. TB agreed to listen to TA's band and offer any advice possible. As TB observed the rehearsal, it was apparent that

TA was trying to use effective methods of instruction. As a matter of fact, TA really did almost all of the right things.

But as the end of the rehearsal neared, TB observed that instead of ending the rehearsal with a brief segment of a piece the band could play well to send the students off with a feeling of accomplishment and pride, TA lectured them on what they hadn't accomplished and how they had to redouble their efforts when they practiced at home, or else the resulting performance would be poor.

After the rehearsal, the veteran TB made a single comment, and then gave TA a piece of advice that made all the difference in the world. "The music you have chosen is not of substantial quality and it is too difficult for your students. I suggest that you assess the skill levels of your students and then find high-quality literature that is matched to these levels. Select high-quality music that is not too easy or too hard based on your assessment."

Before the end of the year, TA had assessed the students' skill levels and had examined a wide range of literature. TA chose some pieces that stretched their abilities and some that they did not have to work as hard to conquer, but TA made sure to choose high-quality music. At the start of a new academic year, the band responded magnificently. TA had overreached on only one selection, which was quickly abandoned. In no time at all, management problems disappeared, the students practiced at home, the group sounded great, and TA ended up leading a band made up of students filled with ever-increasing confidence. In addition, TA found time to engage the ensemble in sight reading exercises at nearly every rehearsal and even had time to begin brief improvisation experiences.

TA led a band, but the same story holds true for any performing ensemble or music class, and demonstrates a critically important area to address. Choosing high-quality literature that is challenging without being beyond the reach of students is a skill that must be developed early in your preparation. Performance difficulties or lack of progress by music classes might be the result of using low-quality literature that is mismatched to the achievement and developmental levels of the students.

It is also important that the *sequence* of concepts and skills you have planned for your students proceeds in step with these levels. It is not easy to match materials, sequence, and developmental levels, but it is worthwhile to spend the time necessary to choose the kinds of high-quality literature that will enrich and propel learning in your classroom.

The value of meaningful, lasting music education comes from your teaching artistry—how you effectively combine high standards of musicianship (not just technical skill but also musicality) with high standards of literature. Choose the literature that allows the time to develop excellence in musicianship and rich musical study. Whether with a performing ensemble or in the music classroom, the literature you choose should allow you the time to work on expressive elements and time to engage your students in sight reading, improvisation, world music, and a variety of musical styles.

How to Select High-Quality Literature

Using the following checklist will help you select high-quality literature for classroom songs, solos, and large or small ensembles. The checklist can also be used for choosing music for directed listening experiences and moving to music activities. Additional resources for choosing high-quality literature appear at the end of this chapter. Note that the checklist does not apply only to the more advanced works. Even very simple works should be examined to determine how the various elements are balanced and how they contribute to the overall effectiveness of the piece. If there is artistic integrity present, the elements will work together to produce a logical and satisfying piece of music, no matter how simple or complex the work.

As a trial experience, select one piece of music from any source and run it through the checklist. As you proceed, write down two to four specific concepts and skills your students will learn as a result of studying and performing the piece, or note how the piece might be used with specific classroom activities. You should also think about how each piece might complement the rest of your students' music study. Upon entering the profession, if you are a classroom music teacher, make sure the music you use with your students works together with the music studied by the band, chorus, or orchestra. If you are a band, chorus, or orchestra teacher, your literature should complement the music studied in the general music classes. If you direct the marching band, jazz choir, jazz band, or musical production, your performance literature should support and enrich the whole music program. Students will benefit by this unified approach that provides reinforcement of concepts and skills.

Important, too, is knowing where the music fits into the longer sequences of instruction. Consider the sequence of classroom study, or the concert and sight reading schedule of repertoire for the semester and the year. Also think about how the music will be effective for a student who completes entire sequences of instruction—for example, the grade groupings: K–4, 5–8, or 9–12.

To help assess the effectiveness of your literature selections applied across these three sequences of study, imagine three students, one with very modest abilities and interest, one with average abilities and interest, and one with high abilities and interest. In your mind, trace the journey of each of these students if they were to travel through these instructional sequences (K–4, 5–8, 9–12). How would they grow musically and what would they learn as a result of these journeys? High-quality literature combined with a well-planned sequence that is implemented across the years can be a powerful component that ties all parts of the program together.

High-Quality Literature Checklist

Carefully review literature, considering the following areas and noting what concepts and skills your students would learn as a result of studying each work.

1. Rhythm and harmony
   - Does the work contain ample rhythmic and harmonic variety to sustain interest?
2. Melody
   - Is the melody interesting? Consider contour, climaxes, and progression (scale, stepwise, repeated). For vocal or choral music, does the melody complement and enhance the text effectively, appropriately, and artistically?
3. Dynamics
   - Is dynamic contrast used for shading to result in enhanced expression?
   - Is dynamic contrast inherent and apparent in the music? Is it indicated with easily understood expressive markings?
4. Ranges
   - Are the ranges and tessitura of the instruments and voices appropriate to the ages and ability levels of the students?
5. Styles and genres
   - Does the work provide opportunities for students to experience a range of styles, historical periods, and genres, as well as musics, languages, or cultures other than their own?
   - How does the music support the use of movement in the music classroom?
   - How does the music support and integrate with the methodologies you are using, such as those developed by Orff, Kodaly, Dalcroze, or Gordon?
6. Appropriateness
   - Does the work complement the overall character of the school community? Particularly consider the lyrics, themes, storyline, and other textual content of choral works, the musical production, and jazz choir.
   - Does the work support and enhance the mission and goals of the music program, school building, and district?

- How does the work fit into a sequence of study that you are building for your students?
- How does it enhance the sequence for the semester, year, and multiyear curriculum?
7. Acknowledged merit
    - Has the work been acknowledged to have merit? From what source? If the work is new, how does it stand up to the scrutiny of the rest of this checklist?
    - Does the work appear on any repertoire lists such as those compiled by states or professional organizations that have a record of regular review and revision?
    - Has the work been recommended by anyone with a recognized track record of success in choosing quality literature? This question is probably the most important and useful one in this checklist. Asking advice from an experienced teacher will help you understand what to look for in choosing quality music that will fit the abilities of your students and function effectively as part of a sequence of study for them.

Further help in your literature search will be provided by getting the sound of quality works in your ears, so you will know what a good piece sounds like. You will graduate from college with the sound of advanced literature in your ears, but make it your business to listen and absorb the sound of high-quality literature from the beginning and middle levels as well.

After using the checklist for reviewing a piece or two, you might think this is a long process to undergo just to find music for your students. It does take time, but using high-quality literature as the basis of your program will act as fertile soil out of which your students will thrive and grow substantially and fruitfully.

Implementing Quality Literature: Problems and Possibilities

In all performing ensemble programs, elementary through high school, as a new teacher you might find that your students have been fed a steady diet of low-quality literature that is really "comic book" or "junk food" music. There is nothing wrong with programming a piece of "fluff" *on occasion*. That practice can help draw parents in, sustain interest, and provide a great deal of fun; however, if the students' diet consists only of this type of music, then any sequence of learning and skills growth is difficult to achieve.

In the elementary classroom or choral area, your students might have been used to singing from word sheets. They may not have seen an octavo piece of choral music until they reached high school, and they might not have experienced the use of classroom instruments of any quality. They might not have been exposed to improvisation and composition, or performed high-quality songs tied to world musics and cultures. Your students might have been used to singing with only their chest voices. They might never have heard how beautiful their natural singing voices are.

If you are faced with a situation that is like either of those described here, you will have to act slowly in weaning the students, parents, other teachers, and administration off this type of diet. Unless you have been hired with the clear expectation that you will immediately revamp the entire program, you might want to wait a year before attempting changes. This will allow you time to build positive connections with your constituent network of parents, fellow teachers, the community, and the administration.

After establishing positive connections with your support network, consider programming a piece or two of high-quality literature that has a rousing tempo and strong rhythm. As you incrementally introduce increasingly weightier music, use student narrators to give brief (four-sentence) introductions that will help the audience understand the pieces better. Make sure you practice with student narrators to help them speak slowly, clearly, and with plenty of volume. Use novel music to change what your listeners have become used to hearing. For example, use music that requires improvisation or scat singing to introduce your students and audience to new approaches.

Keep everyone informed of where your instruction is headed. Just be careful that you do not denigrate what the students were experiencing before, and be careful not to appear condescending. You do not want parents, fellow teachers, and the administration to get the impression that you are a "know-it-all." You simply want to meet the students where they are and expose them to new experiences.

If you determine that your program needs higher-quality literature, take it on as a challenge to find the best examples of music from a variety of genres. In introducing this literature, students will become more engaged with your choices of music if you consistently display a positive demeanor and upbeat teaching attitude. Your encouraging "we can do this" attitude and approach will help sweep your students along to success. As your students progress in basic skills achievement they will gain confidence that feeds on itself. None of this will happen overnight, but little by little, if you persevere in building a program based on the concept of quality, you and your students together will enjoy studying more advanced literature with increasing satisfaction.

Literature Solutions in an Imperfect World

In the real world, your first position most likely will not be as director of a perfectly balanced wind ensemble, orchestra, or chorus. You might be asked to lead an ensemble with very modest abilities, incomplete instrumentation, or lack of students to cover certain parts. For example, you might lack performers to cover the bass line in your band or orchestra, or you might find you have only girls in your middle school chorus. It is apparent you are going to have to recruit students to fill in these gaps; however, what do you do in the meantime? Start by choosing quality music that matches the skill levels of the students that will allow you the time to develop basic skills. As these skills are learned, you can then introduce increasingly more advanced music. For an elementary chorus that has been used to singing only in unison, use rounds and simple two part pieces to introduce harmony and help students learn how to hold parts. For bands and orchestras with incomplete instrumentation, look for pieces that have sufficient doublings to cover missing parts and yet maintain the basic harmonic structure in a pleasing and satisfying way. When faced with a beginning instrumental ensemble, early literature experiences can come from arrangements and compositions that are in band or orchestra method books. These works are a direct outgrowth of valuable basic skills studied in the books. Beginning Suzuki pieces can be effective in combining skills study with performance material. It is important to remember to have the students apply their technical study to concert literature as soon as possible so they can perform in public.

Program Advocacy and Student Retention

Along with building a repertoire of quality literature, you must also continue to strengthen ties with the school community. To advocate for your program, it is very important to "show the world" what your students are gaining by studying music. Try presenting a mini-classroom lesson at a Board of Education meeting. Very briefly explain what concepts and skills the students are learning, and then demonstrate how your students will understand them using one or two activities. Moving to music and singing will provide the public and the district's leaders with a memorable picture of music learning. Follow the classroom lesson with a piece by a performing ensemble and explain how the sequence of instruction interacts between the classroom and the stage. Experience has shown that this approach is very effective in helping the community understand what and how students are learning.

Student retention in all types of performing ensembles can be strengthened by having the students perform often, as soon as they are ready. Parents want to see their children on the stage. So go ahead and arrange for a mini-concert early on for your beginning ensemble. Even if it is a very brief, informal gathering that features one piece, or a part of a piece, it will be well worth it. This strategy is powerful in communicating with parents and encouraging students to stay with the program and keep progressing. I have seen this approach in action.

Early in the year, after the students had only completed a few rehearsals, the teacher invited the parents, families, and friends of his beginning string students to a mini-concert held during the school day to hear just part of a very easy beginning string piece. He personally handed each audience member a small printed program that listed the students' names and then he explained that this performance was a work in progress. He also told the audience what the students had already learned and what he hoped the students would achieve as the year progressed. Then he and the students played the part of the piece they had learned, demonstrating proper posture, bow hold, bow path, and intonation, as well as note and rhythm knowledge. The teacher introduced each student and then had the students repeat the performance. Parents were thrilled at this early evidence of achievement. They had their cameras going full blast and made it clear that they appreciated having their child's first public performance noted on a printed program. The whole mini-performance took about fifteen minutes but resulted in more than a year's worth of goodwill and parent support.

Personal Musical Growth

As part of your teaching artistry, in what ways do you plan on personally growing musically? It is critically important that you keep your own musicality sharp throughout your teaching career. Given the demands of the profession, especially the large amount of paperwork you will encounter, it will be difficult to find the time to keep up on your instrument or stay vocally healthy and "in voice." For vocalists, in particular, you will be using your voice throughout the day, every day, so you will have to develop healthy vocal habits in order to keep up your singing ability.

As difficult as it will be to find the time, if you keep yourself personally involved with making music, your students will be sure to benefit. They will know that you are a "can-do" teacher. If you practice and perform, they will respect you for it. You will find that there is no quieter classroom, chorus, band, or orchestra than when students are listening to a teacher with up-to-date performance skills demonstrate a musical phrase or technique. Join the local symphony chorus, sing or play at church, play clubs, play in the community band or orchestra, and, for a real treat, play or sing at a rehearsal of a colleague's performing group. However you do it, keep your chops up. Your personal performance ability is a powerful teaching tool.

In addition to personal performance, your aural ability will benefit if you regularly hear high-level professional performances. Recordings are second best, but you should make the effort to hear a high-quality professional orchestra, band, vocalist, or choral group in person. Your ears will thank you.

With high-quality literature as the foundation of your classroom or ensemble program, you must now lead the students in learning using your technical knowledge, personal musicality, and command of all of that content from your college music courses.

Mastery of Methods

Effective music teaching combines content with methods to ensure student progress in learning. Methodology is as complex as content and cannot be divorced from it. Methodology includes using in your teaching what you gained from exploring formal methodologies such as the Orff, Kodaly, Dalcroze, Gordon, and Suzuki methodologies. These methodologies are often combined with other approaches learned in elementary and secondary methods courses. Methodology is how you apply to your teaching all of this study and what you have experienced as a performer. It is also crucial to understand that for effective teaching, methodology is intertwined forever with teacher attitude. We will explore that critically important component of effective teaching in a later chapter.

Methodology and Teacher A and Teacher B

We won't attempt to review the content and methods courses from your college experience, but it should be helpful to take a micro-look at methodology from a front-line teaching situation. Let's go back to the tale of TA and TB. It doesn't matter whether new teacher TA was a band, chorus, or orchestra director; veteran teacher TB would have observed the same things. If you remember, TB saw that TA had used a wide range of effective instructional methods. We now identify them. TB noted that TA used the following methods:

- designing a well-thought-out, written lesson plan complete with a clear aim, precise objectives, and a logical procedure;
- placing the lesson outline on the board in advance of the rehearsal;
- consistently getting the ensemble's attention and starting the group with nonverbal cues;
- waiting for silence before speaking and going on;
- giving clear directions when stopping the group;
- knowing and using each student's name;
- always giving a reason for repeating a section of the music;
- giving clear instructions only once;
- maintaining a brisk pace;
- minimizing teacher podium talk;
- asking the students to think about what they just played and having them offer ways to improve specific areas;

- checking up on what has been assigned for home practice by having the students play individually or in small groups;
- giving a home practice assignment for specific areas of need and having the students write it down; and
- trying to be upbeat, positive, and encouraging throughout the rehearsal.

But even though TA used a variety of effective methods, TA still fell short in leading the students to success. TA needed to assess student achievement levels and match them to high-quality literature. It was important that TA sought help and received the right advice from TB. It was also important that TB provided just the right amount of guidance.

If TA had been a classroom music teacher and had chosen poor-quality literature and tried to introduce concepts that were not matched to the development level of the students, TA would have encountered the same sort of frustration and limited student progress even though TA used such effective techniques as the following:

- greeting the students at the door using their names;
- using a variety of group and individual activities that would sustain student interest, provide reinforcement of concepts and skills, and offer opportunities for checking for individual understanding through the transfer of learning;
- maintaining a brisk pace that was aligned with student ability to stay on task;
- minimizing teacher talk and having students learn by doing;
- focusing on just a few concepts and skills rather than using too many that would diffuse the effect of the lesson;
- using a variety of questioning techniques and performing opportunities to check for understanding and provide reinforcement;
- moving about the classroom to vary the physical and psychological learning distance between teacher and students;
- engaging students in music and musical activities from bell to bell; and
- engaging the students in a class-ending summary infused into another activity or by asking various students to "name and explain one thing you learned today."

Effective Collaboration

Happily, TA did achieve growth and success by reaching out to a fellow teacher and heeding the advice. Now TA and TB have continued to share teaching strategies in a group they created of music and nonmusic teachers that meets on Fridays after school at a local coffee shop. As a result of these meetings, they worked out an interdisciplinary project that combined music, art, dance, and social studies. For this project the elementary teachers from the group designed a plan for their students to learn all about a specific culture from the social studies curriculum. They worked with parents, other teachers, and their principals to put on a combined presentation as guests at the high school's annual fine arts showcase. On stage and in the main school lobby, the children highlighted the music, art, dance, and daily life from the culture they had chosen from the social studies curriculum. The community talked about the project in glowing terms long after it took place. The local television station even carried a short piece on the event.

Tuning in to PBS

A few months later, the band, chorus, orchestra, and classroom music teachers in the group thought up a strategy they named "PBS" for teaching the basic skills: Posture, Breathing, Sound. (The orchestra teacher named it "Posture, *Bowing*, Sound" for her ensemble.) They agreed that for one semester they would have their students "tune in" every class to PBS by concentrating on developing those three areas in that order of priority. At the end of the semester, they found out that their students really could understand how posture, breathing (bowing), and sound affected each other by working in sequence. The students also demonstrated understanding by effectively applying their improved skills in these three areas to the classroom song literature and the concert literature. Other teachers in the district heard of the PBS initiative, used it themselves, and also experienced positive results.

Sharing Ideas

TA, TB, and the teacher coffee group might not exist exactly as they appear here, but all across the country, teachers are constantly working together combining all the content knowledge they possess, method ideas, performance experiences, and personal musicianship to find ways to help their students grow musically. All of their knowledge, ideas, projects, and plans have the potential to provide all types of students with blue chip musical experiences.

Summary

In this chapter you noted the importance of knowing your subject matter thoroughly (command of content) and you explored the importance of building a sequence of study that is strongly linked to national standards and student achievement levels. You also examined the essential content element of quality literature for performance or use in the music classroom—its selection and implementation. Program advocacy, student retention, and personal musical growth were then highlighted as necessary elements of teaching artistry. After command of content, you examined mastery of methods that included techniques for effective classroom techniques to aid in lesson implementation. A scenario depicting effective collaboration ended the chapter.

In the next chapter you will apply your content and methods knowledge to developing effective instructional plans and procedures. This critically important area is where the rubber meets the road. The next chapter will help you answer the questions, "How well will you be able to design and implement sequential, practical lesson plans that will enable your students to progress in attaining growth in content and skills understanding?" "How well will you be able to assess the results of student learning?" and "How will you manage your classroom and include all types of learners in your day-to-day instruction?"

For Reflection, Discussion, Assignment

1. Review the MENC National Standards for Music Education and see how they align with the accompanying Achievement Standards by accessing www.menc.org > Resources > Online Publications > *The National Music Education Standards (The School Music Program: A New Vision).* As a result of your review of the standards, choose one standard for grades K–4 and two companion achievement standards, and explain what activities you might use that will lead students to meet those two achievement standards. If appropriate to the activity, discuss what quality literature you might use to support the activity.

2. As in question 1, choose one standard for grades 5–8 and two companion achievement standards, and explain what activities you might use that will lead students to meet those two achievement standards. If appropriate to the activity, discuss what quality literature you might use to support the activity.

3. As in question 1, choose one standard for grades 9–12 and two companion achievement standards, and explain what activities you might use that will lead students to meet those two achievement standards. If appropriate to the activity, discuss what quality literature you might use to support the activity.

4. Access www.menc.org > Resources > Online Publications > *Performance Standards for Music K–12.* In the K–4 section, choose one standard with accompanying performance standard, and provide one strategy for helping a student move from the Basic to the Proficient level.

5. Apply the same process from question 4 to the grades 5–8 section of the Performance Standards.
6. Apply the same process from question 4 to the grades 9–12 section of the Performance Standards.
7. Using the high-quality literature checklist from this chapter, identify three high-quality works for either elementary, middle, or high school, and explain why these works pass the test for high-quality literature. Choose music from the following resources, from state lists, or from music publisher catalogs. Or use works suggested by an in-service music teacher.
8. Using the checklist, identify a different set of three high-quality works that you could use as a *sequence* of study for band, chorus, or orchestra at the elementary, middle, or high school levels. Choose one piece for K–4, one for 5–8, and one for 9–12. Identify the sequence of concepts and skills the students will learn as a result of performing this literature, and how each work aligns with the achievement standards for each level (K–4, 5–8, 9–12). Choose music from the following resources, from state lists, or from music publisher catalogs. Or use works suggested by an in-service music teacher.
9. Explain how you are personally growing as a musician and how you intend to continue growing throughout your professional life.
10. With permission, observe an in-service music teacher. Report on and be prepared to discuss three to five teaching techniques or strategies you observed that you believe were effective in causing students to learn. Use the tale of Teacher A and Teacher B as a guide. If you were the teacher, what would you have done differently to cause students to learn?

Resources

Anderson, William M., and Joy E. Lawrence. *Integrating Music into the Elementary Classroom*, 8th ed. Belmont, CA: Thomson Learning, 2009.

Apfelstadt, Hilary. "First Things First: Selecting Repertoire." *Music Educators Journal* 87, no. 1 (July 2000): 19–22, 46.

Bauer, William I. "Classroom Management for Ensembles." *Music Educators Journal* 87, no. 6 (May 2001): 27–32.

Blackstone, Jerry, Janet Galvan, Ann Howard Jones, James Jordan, Libby Larsen, Heather J. Buchanan, and Matthew W. Mehaffey. *Teaching Music through Performance in Choir*, vol. 2. Chicago: GIA, 2007.

Buchanan, Heather J., and Matthew W. Mehaffey, eds. *Teaching Music through Performance in Choir*, vol. 1. Chicago: GIA, 2005.

Campbell, Patricia Shehan. *Musician and Teacher: An Orientation to Music Education*. New York: W. W. Norton, 2008.

Campbell, Patricia Shehan, and Carol Scott Kassner. *Music in Childhood*, 3rd ed. New York: Schirmer, 2009.

Choksy, Lois, Robert M. Abramson, Avon E. Gillespie, David Woods, and Frank York. *Teaching Music in the Twenty-First Century*, 2nd ed. Upper Saddle River, NJ: Prentice-Hall, 2001.

Colwell, Richard J., and Michael Hewitt. *Teaching of Instrumental Music*, 4th ed. Upper Saddle River, NJ: Prentice-Hall, 2010.

Evertson, Carolyn, M., and Edmund T. Emmer. *Classroom Management for Elementary Teachers*, 8th ed. Boston: Allyn & Bacon, 2008.

Haugland, Susan L. *Crowd Control: Classroom Management and Effective Teaching for Chorus, Band and Orchestra*. Lanham, MD: Rowman & Littlefield/MENC: The National Association for Music Education, 2007.

Littrel, David, ed. *Teaching Music through Performance in Orchestra*, vols. 2 and 3. Chicago: GIA, 2003, 2008.

Littrell, David, and Laura Reed Racin, eds. *Teaching Music through Performance in Orchestra*, vol. 1. Chicago: GIA, 2001.

MENC: The National Association for Music Education. *Performance Standards for Music: Strategies and Benchmarks for Assessing Progress Toward the National Standards, Grades PreK–12*. Reston, VA: MENC, 1996.

———. *The School Music Program: A New Vision*. Reston, VA: MENC, 1994.

Merrion, Margaret. "Classroom Management for Beginning Music Educators." *Music Educators Journal* 78, no. 2 (October 1991): 53–56.

Miles, Richard, ed. *Teaching Music through Performance in Band*, 7 vols. Chicago: GIA, 1998–2009.

———, ed. *Teaching Music through Performance in Beginning Band*, vol. 2. Chicago: GIA, 2008.

———, ed. *Teaching Music through Performance in Jazz*. Chicago: GIA, 2008.

———, ed. *Teaching Music through Performing Marches*. Chicago: GIA, 2003.

Miles, Richard, and Thomas Dvorak, eds. *Teaching Music through Performance in Beginning Band*, vol. 1. Chicago: GIA, 2001.

Moore, Marvelene C. *Classroom Management in General, Choral, and Instrumental Music Programs*. With Angela L. Batey and David M. Royse. Lanham, MD: Rowman & Littlefield Education, 2002.

Persellin, Diane. "The Importance of High-Quality Literature." *Music Educators Journal* 87, no. 1 (July 2000): 17–18.

Phillips, Kenneth H. *Directing the Choral Music Program*. New York: Oxford University Press, 2004.

Rosene, Paul E. "10 Tips for Discovering High-Quality Music for Your Band or Orchestra." *Teaching Music* 11, no. 5 (April 2004): 34.

Spaeth, Jeanne. "Finding Quality Literature for Young Children." *Teaching Music* 2, no. 1 (August 1994): 40–41.

Townsend, Alfred S. "Bands of Excellence Tune in to PBS: Posture, Breathing, Sound." *National Band Association Journal* 48, no. 3 (May 2008): 49–51.

———. "Driving Music Education: Who's at the Wheel?" *Teaching Music* 16, no. 1 (August 2008): 30–32.

———. "Recharge Your Battery: Ideas for a More Musical and Integrated Concert Band Percussion Section." *National Band Association Journal* 47, no. 3 (May 2002): 45–46.

———. "Stop! Look! Listen! for Effective Band Rehearsals." *Teaching Music* 10, no. 4 (February 2003): 22–25.

———. "With Great Sounds to Match Student Bands Will Improve." *The Instrumentalist* 57, no. 8 (March 2003): 29–34.

3

Effective Instruction

All of the content and methodology knowledge in the world will not mean much unless you are successful in organizing instruction so that students will have sequential, productive learning experiences. What follows are essential planning components and a process for using them in designing and implementing lessons, and assessing student learning. Techniques are also provided for classroom management that will increase your effectiveness. Using the material studied in this chapter, you will be able to construct practical lesson plans that can be understood by music and nonmusic administrators, and that will enable you to explain to parents, fellow teachers, and administrators what you are teaching, why you are teaching it, and how you will assess student progress. In addition, information is provided for teaching students with diverse learning needs. The chapter ends with ways your teaching will be officially evaluated by school administrators.

Practical Planning

There are many ways to plan for instruction, but whatever approach is used, careful long- and short-range planning is essential to effective teaching. I have never met an effective teacher who did not consistently engage in the thoughtful planning of instruction *sequenced* within each lesson, from lesson to lesson, and from unit to unit. These effective teachers share a common planning process as they think about how they lead their students in learning. This process includes the following:

1. considering previous learning and identifying the existing achievement levels of each student and the class;

2. selecting specific content to be studied that matches these achievement levels;
3. specifying the aim of the lesson along with the construction of meaningful and measurable lesson objectives that satisfy the lesson aim and raise student achievement levels;
4. considering how each student will meet the objectives;
5. preparing sequenced learning activities and experiences that result in purposeful learning involving knowledge, understanding, and skills;
6. assessing individual and group achievement; and
7. using these assessments as a teaching tool to reinforce concepts and skills, and to affect future lessons.

This process can be easily applied to daily, unit, or longer-range planning. Later in this chapter you will see how this process works in constructing lesson plans.

Experienced teachers are adept at constructing effective units of study and daily lessons because they draw on a bank of ideas and plans that they have developed over the years. They use their own creativity along with information gleaned from research, professional literature, conference sessions, and discussions with other educators. Through these same avenues, you can look forward to developing your own bank of effective lessons.

As you enter the profession, you must be able to construct and implement daily lessons that not only enable your students to learn how to learn but also are precise, concise, and understandable by others, such as non-music administrators who might evaluate your teaching. All administrators know the essentials of effective planning, but many do not possess intimate knowledge of music and music learning. So your planning must be written clearly, avoiding jargon and excessive technical terms.

Keep in mind that your lesson plans are the written record of your day-to-day teaching. Of course, the plans you construct will provide invaluable direction to your teaching. They provide you, your students, and administrators with a "road map" of the learning journey that will take place in your classroom. However, plans serve other functions. These plans, along with classroom evaluations from your supervisors, are major components in determining whether you will keep your job and eventually be awarded tenure. In many instances, the daily lessons contained in your plan book must be submitted to your building administrator each week throughout the academic years until you receive tenure. The plan books of tenured faculty are usually evaluated less often. So it is critically important that your daily and unit planning be very carefully prepared and well written. Your job may depend on it.

It is important to note, however, that it is quite possible to plan and construct lessons on paper that satisfy the components of educational theory without having the planning result in enduring, meaningful learning. The effectiveness of any lesson plan should be measured by how well the lesson engages the students, raises achievement levels, and provides for future growth and involvement in the discipline.

In order to know what the content and achievement expectations are, remember the standards set by MENC that outline what all students should experience in school music programs, and remember the accompanying Achievement Standards that provide sequential examples for addressing each of the standards across the grade levels. But how do you know if your students have met those standards? For that information, recall the MENC Performance Standards that contain assessment strategies and descriptions of student responses at three levels—basic, proficient, and advanced. Use this information to give purpose and power to your lesson planning and instruction.

In all lesson and unit planning it is critically important to strive to go beyond the mere collecting of facts about music. Lesson plans that are based merely on naming and listing activities are dead-end approaches. After the naming and listing, what does the student do with that information? Meaningful learning is more likely to take place if the gaining of factual knowledge is set within a sequence of lessons. These lessons should enable students to effectively apply their knowledge to new activities and learning situations while helping them make reasoned aesthetic judgments. Providing enduring musical experiences is unlikely to occur if you stick to the old concept of viewing students' heads as hollow vessels that the teacher fills with information.

Many years ago George Katona got it right when he wrote that the most effective teaching methods were those that enabled students to "learn to learn—they should not merely learn to memorize—they should learn to learn by understanding."[1] Effective teachers of today support this claim by using multiple teaching approaches to increase student understanding that include engaging their students in learning by doing.

Your lesson planning and implementation should provide all students with a range of ways to understand. As an example, for an elementary lesson on steady beat connected to reading quarter- and eighth-note rhythms, student understanding will be increased if you use more approaches than just referring to a note value diagram. Multiple teaching approaches will maintain interest and help students internalize the concepts and skills of the lesson. These approaches might include discovering examples of steady beat in the school and at home, counting and clapping combinations of rhythms over a steady beat, and moving to music activities. Reinforcement of rhythm reading can be provided by having students sing songs that use their knowledge of steady beat and quarter- and eighth-note rhythms. Student conductors for these activities can also be used to add another way for learners to understand how steady beat relates to combinations of rhythms. Effective teachers are always on the prowl to find additional ways for their students to experience concepts and skills.

Studying educational theory provides a critically important foundation for the profession; however, of equal importance is the ability to apply the theory to precise, practical lesson plans that enable students to learn to learn. The ultimate goal is to enable your students to function independently so they can continue learning beyond their school years.

The following process and lesson plan format can be easily adjusted to satisfy planning procedures required by your school district or building.

The Planning Process

Lesson design need not be a complex or arduous process. The process presented here has proven to function well in a variety of teaching situations. Additional sources for lesson design and implementation appear at the end of this chapter in the resources.

The lesson plan structure that follows contains ample specific detail. There are other types of plans that require less detail; however, once you have become familiar with the more detailed plan provided here, you will be able to adapt to those that are more general. What follows are two lesson plan formats. The first is useful for classroom instruction. The second applies to ensemble rehearsals. Both formats use the same concepts of planning and implementation.

Writing a practical lesson plan is not difficult if you break the process down into a series of questions and answers.

Before writing any lesson plan, ask yourself:

1. How does this lesson function as part of the sequence of study planned for the unit?
2. How does this lesson fit in to what will be meaningful and enduring for students to learn over the long haul?
3. How will this lesson help students learn to learn—to become independent learners?
4. How does this lesson integrate with study in other disciplines? Note: It is not reasonable to expect that every lesson integrate with some other discipline; however, this question should always be considered as you plan. Some schools require documentation of such integration.

Then recall the planning process from earlier in the chapter. This sequence consists of the following steps:

1. Consider previous learning and identify the existing achievement levels of each student and the class.
2. Select specific content to be studied that matches these achievement levels.

3. Specify the aim of the lesson along with the construction of meaningful and measurable lesson objectives that satisfy the lesson aim and raise student achievement levels.
4. Consider how each student will meet the objectives.
5. Prepare sequenced learning activities and experiences that result in purposeful learning involving knowledge, understanding, and skills.
6. Assess individual and group achievement.
7. Use these assessments as a teaching tool to reinforce concepts and skills and to affect future lessons.

This process is demonstrated in the following sample middle school lesson plan, which engages students in composing a sound portrait of mood using brass instrument sounds. Using questions and answers you will see how the process plays out.

Sample Lesson Plan 1: Classroom Music

1. What Is the Overall Aim of the Lesson?

Aim

Construct the aim as part of the planned unit of study (multiple sequential lessons). Base the aim on knowledge and understanding from previous lessons, and keep in mind what the next lesson should be. For example, the aim of a middle school lesson using brass instrument sounds to compose sound portraits should take into consideration that in previous lessons the students have been introduced to the brass family and the concepts of color, dynamics, register, and tempo. Students also have learned how to use MIDI keyboards, computers, and software to create compositions.

Our sample brass lesson aim is to compose a sound portrait that effectively depicts mood using sampled brass instrument sounds and the concepts of color, dynamics, register, and tempo.

2. What Should I Expect Each Student To Be Able To Do as a Result of This Lesson?

Objectives

For each lesson, write two to four objectives that are precise and measurable. Avoid using words that are open to multiple interpretations. For instance, avoid forming objectives that start with the following phrases:

- To enjoy
- To appreciate
- To feel
- To grasp the significance of
- To believe

Rather, begin your objectives with words that are more precise, such as the following:

- To compare and contrast
- To define and describe
- To perform accurately
- To identify and differentiate
- To name and apply
- To compose and analyze

As an example, for our middle school lesson on composing portraits using brass instrument sounds, you might construct the following objectives:

Objectives: Students will be able to . . .

- Define terms and describe examples of brass color, dynamics, register, and tempo.
- Compare, contrast, and discuss the use of brass instrument sounds to reflect mood.
- Effectively apply knowledge of brass color, dynamics, register, and tempo to the use of sampled sounds to create portraits of moods chosen by the class.

3. What Will Be the Content of This Lesson That Will Address the Stated Objectives?

Content

Include here a brief synopsis of the main body of information of the lesson. For example, for our sample middle school composition lesson, the content might include the following:

- recorded examples of works using brass to depict mood through color, dynamics, register, and tempo;
- samples of brass sounds from a quality digital sampling keyboard.

4. What Materials Will I Need for Delivering the Content of This Lesson?

Materials

For our brass instrument composition lesson, materials include CDs and player, MIDI keyboard, computer with composition program, and a sound portrait template on board and in handouts for home use.

5. What Procedure Will I Use to Result in Student Understanding and Meet the Lesson Objectives? Is This Lesson Integrated with Any Other Subject Area? If So, How Will I Address This Integration in the Procedure Section?

Procedure

Use the procedure outline that follows to focus the learning process. Remember that you have only forty minutes, on average, for a middle school class session. The typical new teacher tries to cover too much material in this time span, thus losing the focus of the lesson. By trying to cover too much material you will also not have enough time to check for individual and group understanding, and you will not have enough time to provide for the questioning that should take place throughout the lesson. You also will not have time to conduct a meaningful class-ending summary or to tell the students what the next lesson will be. With any class, it is more effective to concentrate on meeting only a few objectives to satisfy the aim of the lesson, and using a variety of activities to reinforce these few areas.

In addition, as you construct the procedure section make sure you keep in mind the following important components you will use as you teach the lesson.

- *Modeling* is the demonstration of skills and concepts by teacher and students.
- Reinforcement of learning is accomplished through consistent checking for individual and group understanding by questioning and performance, and by applying skills and concepts to new situations (transfer of knowledge and learning). This section is critically important as it provides students with experience in learning how to learn.
- Lesson linkages connect the lesson segments so each segment builds on previous knowledge and leads smoothly to the next segment.

Procedure Outline

Review   Briefly review the concepts of color, dynamics, register, and tempo using questioning and recorded brass instrument works.

New   Introduce the concept of composing sound portraits of mood.
Activity 1   Using recorded examples of brass music, students identify,
               define, and describe connections between brass instrument
               sounds and mood. Students discuss how color, dynamics,
               register, and tempo affect mood.
Activity 2   Using a MIDI keyboard, computer, and composition pro-
               gram, students as a class discuss and apply knowledge
               of color, dynamics, register, and tempo to the creation
               of a fifteen-second brass sound portrait of a mood they
               choose such as angry and agitated, sad and mournful, or
               happy and joyful. Students select colors, dynamics, regis-
               ters, and tempos. The portraits are then sketched on the
               board by selected students using a template that indicates
               color (which brass instruments are used); dynamics (soft,
               medium-loud, loud, crescendo, decrescendo); register
               (high, medium, low); and tempo (slow, medium fast, fast).
               Teacher or selected students input the sketched composi-
               tion into the composition program and play it back. Stu-
               dents determine the effectiveness of the composition in
               capturing the mood, suggest modifications, input those
               changes and play it back again. If time permits, students
               create another composition.

Summary

The class-ending summary should not be a lecture, nor should it be too long.
Be sure to engage the students in your summary by having them analyze
and respond to what they have learned. An effective summary strategy for
this composition lesson is to ask students to identify and describe how a
single brass instrument of their choice could express one single mood.

6. How Will I Assess Student Understanding and Achievement of the Lesson Objectives?

Assessment

For assessing student achievement relative to the daily lesson plan, use an
assessment guide (see example later in this chapter) that is directly linked
to your lesson objectives. By so doing, your lessons will have a productive
focus. As Connie L. Hale and Susan K. Green note, "Targeting the end result
provides a clear image of what you ultimately want to achieve in your instruction. A concrete mental image of what needs to be accomplished comes
before trying to accomplish it. With clear goals, you can easily capitalize
on the teaching potential of music and materials."[2] However, care must be

taken in selecting activities and materials to propel the lesson procedure. As Hale and Green state,

> Research confirms that attempts to incorporate engaging or interesting materials should always be viewed in the context of targeted outcomes. . . . In our experience beginning teachers often select music and classroom activities based on what engages their interest or what they think students will enjoy. While music should engender enthusiasm, equally valuable is the innate teaching potential in a piece or activity. . . . In fact, most assessment experts recommend that you design your instruction and your assessment at the same time so that they are consistent and reinforce each other. Evaluation can be intertwined with the lesson and reinforce its goal.[3]

As part of the assessment process, it can be instructive to ask the class to rate themselves based on the assessment guide you create. You will find that the students are really tough on themselves in this activity. For our brass composition lesson, you and the class might assess the effectiveness of the lesson by asking, "How accurately and fully did individuals and the class define, identify and describe brass color, dynamics, register, and tempo? How effectively did the class apply their knowledge of brass color, dynamics, register, and tempo to the portrait composed by the group?" These questions can be codified by using the following assessment guide.

The Assessment Guide

The purpose of an assessment guide (sometimes called a *rubric* or *scoring guide*) is to provide students, parents, teachers, and administrators with the areas that will be assessed and what the ratings mean. For example, a parent should know exactly what a grade of B stands for on the report card or assignment. Parents and students can then work more effectively to raise the grade. Assessment guides can also help you rate your own lessons. It is important that the results of this and any assessment be used to evaluate your teaching and affect modifications in such areas as lesson content (e.g., musical selections, level of difficulty), activities, lesson pace, modeling, checking for understanding, transfer of knowledge and learning, and linkages among lesson components.

A common approach to constructing an assessment guide is to use a five-point system. This guide uses a rating of 5 as the highest achievement level and a rating of 1 as the lowest. What follows is an example of an assessment guide for our sample composition lesson. This sample guide can be adapted to suit many different assessment applications.

Middle School Composition Lesson Sample Assessment Guide

Note that this is a sample assessment guide for *class* achievement. This guide would be helpful in determining the effectiveness of the lesson in relation to the overall class. For individual achievement assessment, you would use the same guide, substituting a child's name in place of "Students."

5 = Students were able to define, identify, and describe completely and accurately brass color, dynamics, register, and tempo, using examples to support their responses. Students demonstrated superior understanding of these components by using them to create extraordinarily effective sound portraits of moods.

4 = Students were able to define, identify, and describe many aspects of brass color, dynamics, register, and tempo. Students demonstrated satisfactory understanding of these components by using them to create effective sound portraits of moods.

3 = Students were able to define, identify, and describe some aspects of brass color, dynamics, register, and tempo. Students demonstrated some understanding of these components by using them to create somewhat effective sound portraits of moods.

2 = Students were able to define, identify, and describe only a few aspects of brass color, dynamics, register, and tempo. Students demonstrated limited understanding of these components by using them unevenly to create sound portraits of moods.

1 = Students were not able to define, identify, and describe any aspects of brass color, dynamics, register, and tempo. Students did not demonstrate understanding of these components by being unable to use them to create sound portraits of moods.

This assessment guide can easily translate into letter grades. 5 = A; 4 = B; 3 = C; 2 = D; 1 = F

7. What Standards Will Be Addressed by This Lesson?

Standards Addressed

Based on the content of your lesson, identify by number the national, state, or local standards addressed and include a few words that characterize the standards referenced. For example, if your lesson focused on creating sound portraits using brass instrument sounds, you would list the following:

National

MENC National Standards for Music Education
#4 Composing and arranging music within specified guidelines

State

Identify here state state standard(s) addressed

8. What Are the Expectations for the Next Lesson and Home Study?

Next Lesson and Assignment

At home, students use the sound portrait template handouts to create a sound portrait sketch of one mood of their choice. For example, mood (sad); color (trombone, tuba); dynamics (soft); register (low); and tempo (slow). For extra credit they can create two sketches that reflect two different moods. For the next class, students will use an electronic keyboard to add sound to the sketches. Students will also discuss the effectiveness of their compositions and be introduced to the concept of form by using contrasting moods to create two- and three-part compositions.

The sample middle school composition lesson plan shown on page 47 uses the structure as shown in the following template. Enter this template into your computer so you do not have to rewrite the plan outline each time you prepare a lesson. This template can be easily modified to suit the requirements of your school.

Sample Lesson Plan 2: Ensemble Rehearsal

Sample lesson plan 2 contains basic planning elements common to both the music classroom and the ensemble rehearsal. However, the format is slightly different from lesson plan 1 in order to address ensemble rehearsal issues.

You will note that lesson plan 2 begins with an *Aim/Do Now* section. The *Do Now* lesson element can also be used in the music classroom. This element contains content and an activity related directly to the day's lesson. It is usually written on the board so students can get to work on it individually right away without any instruction from the teacher.

The *objectives* are clearly articulated and are formed according to what students will be able to do as a result of the lesson. The objectives are based on the accurate execution of selected concepts and skills taken from the listing provided in the lesson template. You may find that nonmusic administrators, in particular, will be interested in and impressed by this list of content and skills the students are addressing as they rehearse. The idea is to show administrators and others that your students are not just playing or singing pieces; they are studying and learning from them.

Daily Lesson Plan Template: Classroom Music

Teacher Name _____   Date _____

School Building _____

Grade/Class _____

Lesson Plan

Unit Title: _____

Previous Lesson

Today's Lesson

1. **Aim***

2. **Objectives***

   Students Will Be Able to (SWBAT):

   -
   -
   -
   -

3. **Content**

4. **Materials**

5. **Procedure**

   Activity 1

   Activity 2

   Activity 3

6. **Assessment**

7. **Standards Addressed**

   National

   State

8. **Next Lesson and Assignment**

*These lesson components can be used if your school requires a short form of daily lesson plans.

The *procedure* begins by linking the warm up and technical study to the performance literature study through the use of a common key and similar concepts and skills. In other words, the ensemble will apply directly to the performance literature what they studied in the warm up and technical skills portion of the lesson. The procedure section follows the pattern of reviewing the material from the previous rehearsal, checking for understanding of the assignment through individual and sectional performances, introducing new literature, giving the assignment, and ending the rehearsal with a performance of a short portion of the literature that the group can play or sing well. By ending the rehearsal in this way the students will go on their way with increased confidence in their performance potential.

The *assessment* and *standards addressed* sections are the same as in sample lesson plan 1.

For a template of this lesson plan, enter only the bolded items into your computer.

This sample plan for high school concert band can be readily adapted for orchestra or chorus at any level.

Teacher Name: Your Name   **School Building:** Your Senior High School
Ensemble: Concert Band 9–12   **Date:** XXXX

1. Aim/Do Now

Aim: Accurately perform technical study #15 from the warm-up book and selected portions of the concert literature.
Do Now: Students individually study warm-up book exercise #15. Focus: notes, rhythms, accidentals.

2. Objectives: Students will be able to . . .

Concepts and skills to be studied will be selected from: focus, posture, breathing, tone quality, intonation, blend, balance, dynamics, articulation, bowing (orchestra), diction (chorus), phrasing, notes, rhythms, key signature, accidentals, meter changes, expression, ensemble precision.

- Sight read and perform accurately sixteenth-note rhythms, accidentals, and notes of warm-up book exercise #15 (key of E-flat major).
- Competently apply notes, rhythms, and key signature (E-flat major) of warm up to introduction section of *March*.

- Accurately perform concepts and skills in assigned portions of the concert literature. Today's emphasis: ensemble precision, tone, intonation, dynamics (accents).
- Analyze and sight read new portion of concert literature.

3. Procedure

Warm Up/Technical Study

Warm Ups for Concert Band #15 (Key of E-Flat Major)
   Analyze, sight read. Students and teacher assess achievement, identify areas for improvement, replay, and reassess achievement. Emphasis: notes, rhythms, accidentals, dynamics (accents).

Performance Literature Study: Review and New

   Review assignment (RA): *March* introduction and first strain (key of E-flat major).
   Check for understanding through individual and sectional performances.
   RA: *Dance #1*
   Rehearsal marks:
      B–C woodwind runs: ensemble precision, note and rhythm accuracy.
      E–F brass punctuations: tone, dynamics, intonation.
      E–F percussion motifs: dynamics (accents), ensemble precision.
   New: *Ballad #1*
   Analyze: (teacher and students talk through the work's "road map" and selected areas of rhythm, dynamics and accidentals).
   Sight read: teacher and students assess (discuss areas in need of improvement), and replay.
   End: *March*: coda

4. Assignment

Additional concepts and skills to be selected by conductor and students

   Dance #1
   Rehearsal marks and performers
      B–C, D–E: Woodwinds
      F–G: Brass and mallets
      Emphasis: Rhythmic accuracy
   Ballad #1
      Intro B: Everyone
      D–G: Solo line
      Emphasis: Note accuracy, phrasing, dynamics

March
   Transition H: Everyone
   Trio: Woodwinds
   Emphasis: Notes, rhythms, accidentals, accents

5. Assessment

To what degree did students achieve the objectives as stated previously in step 2?

6. Standards Addressed

National

   MENC National Standards for Music Education
   #2 Performing on instruments, alone and with others, a varied repertoire
      of music.
   #7 Evaluating music and music performances.

State

   Identify here state standard(s) addressed

Lesson Implementation

It is fine and dandy to design beautiful lessons on paper, but if the proposed plan is not effectively implemented, the well-crafted lesson is useless. The old saying "Well, I taught 'em but they didn't learn" ignores the purpose of instruction—learning. Help your students understand by using a variety of activities to reinforce a few clearly articulated skills and concepts. Check for individual and group understanding, and provide reinforcement of the lesson content through questioning, quizzes, individual and sectional performances, and the regular application of skills and concepts to new learning situations (transfer of knowledge and learning).

Above all, keep in mind the importance of your attitude in the learning process. Creative lesson plans, superior content knowledge, the latest materials, and a state-of-the-art facility mean little if you are not able to communicate effectively with your students. Ask yourself, "How effectively am I connecting with my students? Are my actions matching my words? Am I teaching what I deeply believe and am passionate about? Am I emulating those attitudes used by the teachers that made a difference in my life?" If you can provide positive responses to these questions, you are well on your way to interacting meaningfully and honestly with your students. As you proceed through this book, you will continue to fine-tune your personal combination of content, methods, and attitude that will help you develop as an effective music teacher.

Classroom and Ensemble Management

In the article "Evidence-based Practices in Classroom Management: Considerations for Research to Practice," by Brandi Simonsen and colleagues, we read, "Classroom management is an important element of pre-service teacher training and in-service behavior and is comprised of three central components: maximized allocation of time for instruction, arrangement of instructional activities to maximize academic engagement and achievement, and proactive behavior management practices."[4]

Undergirding these three components of classroom management is the foundation of effective organization, preparation, and planning.

William I. Bauer notes in an article on ensemble management, "Teachers skilled in classroom management, regardless of the subject area, are proactive. They understand that a well-managed classroom is often the result of good planning and preparation."[5] A well-planned lesson that is taught at a brisk pace can minimize many management issues. If you allow too much "down time," students may fill the time with activities of their own. That is why it is critically important to have all materials and equipment all ready to go in plenty of time before class. For example, do you know how to operate the electronic equipment? Is the CD or DVD all cued up?

If you are a teacher who goes from classroom to classroom or building to building, you have to be extra organized in order to maximize instructional time. The use of different colored crates for various classes or buildings can help you save time. For example, red crates can be designated for fourth grade, Building A, and so on.

At all times, try to anticipate problems that might interfere with student time on task. Here is an example from real life. A teacher had ordered a technology workstation to be delivered on the day she was to teach a fifth-grade electronic music lesson. At the last minute, the technician dutifully delivered the equipment but had neglected to bring an extension cord (the only usable outlet was far away). The savvy teacher always kept a long extension cord on her cart for just such situations. The problem was solved and no instructional time was lost.

For all music classrooms, having the learning space well organized ahead of time creates an atmosphere conducive to productive behavior. If students enter a classroom that is in disarray, their behavior could very well reflect the condition of the room. It really makes a positive difference if from the very first day of school, the students enter a clean classroom that has the furniture usefully and neatly aligned, the materials, equipment and instruments organized, the rules posted, and the lesson plan outline on the board.

Classroom Structure and Time Management

A well-structured opening and closing lesson procedure will help you manage time and student behavior. If your students know that every class starts with a brief "Do Now" activity that is placed on the board in advance of class, they will get focused sooner and be less likely to waste time chatting among themselves. For all classes and rehearsals stand at the door and greet the students. This simple act sets the tone for the entire class time. For the music classroom you will save time, while providing an immediate musical experience, by using "entering music" to play the students into their seats. Your lesson will be enriched if this music corresponds with the day's lesson.

Excessive teacher talk can distract from student focus. Avoid telling stories unrelated to the lesson, or pontificating at length from the podium. Instead, increase the regular use of nonverbal cues. These silent cues will improve focus, save time, and thus reduce opportunities for side conversations or other distractions. For the general music classroom, you can train your students to become silent when you raise your hand with the first two fingers extended in a "V." Have the students lift their hands in like fashion and become silent. To have the class line up, play "lining up" music that is high, soft, staccato tip-toeing music (you don't want to send them out of your room in an excited, noisy state). This lining up music can sometimes be linked to the concepts and skills studied in the day's lesson.

For a choral group nonverbal cue, play two notes on the piano in succession such as an upward perfect fifth, meaning "All Stand" and the reverse "All Sit." Other nonverbal musical cues can help you save your voice and increase time efficiency. For "boys sing only," use a low register cue on the piano; for "girls only," use a high register cue. I am sure you can come up with additional nonverbal cues.

For all ensembles, students can learn to become silent when you step behind the piano, music stand, or step up on the podium. In conducting, avoid "counting off" to start the ensemble. If you count off, students won't watch you. Simply step behind the music stand or mount the podium for silence, indicate the tempo, raise your baton or hands, and give a breath beat and start beat. Your students will soon learn to watch. You don't count off in concert, so there is no need to do it in rehearsal. The exception is for jazz groups, for which you establish the groove and style with the rhythm section, and then the overall group, before counting off to start the tune. Jazz groups for the most part are self-conducted by means of the rhythm section after you kick off the piece.

I know of one band director who occasionally holds silent rehearsals in which no one, neither the students nor the teacher, speaks from bell to bell. The rehearsal outline is on the board, opening and closing routines are well established, and the conductor uses prearranged hand signals to indicate directions. As a result, his students become quite adept at ensemble focus.

Managing Student Behavior

In addition to the management techniques and ideas described previously, it is important that you establish a code of behavior for your class or rehearsal space at the beginning of the school year. Before the first day of school, post three to five behavior rules (not twenty!) that are in line with the rules of the department and the school. There are general rules that need further explanation such as "Be polite and respect others." And there are more specific rules that require less explanation such as "Be in your seat ready to participate when the bell rings." As a new teacher, you might want to have one or two general rules, followed by three specific ones. The general rules will require students to think about their behavior relative to a number of situations, while the specific rules will provide clear direction in targeted areas. Engage the students and reinforce their understanding by having them explain what they think each rule means.

As stated by Harry K. Wong and Rosemary T. Wong in the book *The First Days of School*, "The function of a rule is to prevent or encourage behavior by clearly stating student expectations."[6] They further state,

> Students must know from the very beginning how they are expected to behave and work in a classroom work environment. Discipline dictates how they are to behave, and procedures and routines dictate how they are to work. . . . Since a procedure is how you want something done, it is the responsibility of the teacher to have procedures clearly stated. A routine is what the student does automatically without prompting or supervision. Thus a routine becomes a habit, practice, or custom for the student.[7]

A procedure for a music class might focus on what to do at the start or end of every lesson, what to do in collecting or distributing materials or instruments, or what to do when the conductor steps up on the podium. Review the rules and their consequences more than once with your students, and consistently and fairly apply them. Go over procedures many times until they become routines. As noted in *The First Days of School*, "Every class needs to have a set of procedures. Procedures allow the class to operate smoothly. A smooth-running, effective class is free of confusion and is a pleasure to teach and learn in."[8]

In establishing your classroom-management system, it is important to stay connected to all parts of your students' school and home life. To do this, make sure parents, fellow teachers, and the administration know what your rules and consequences are. It is equally important to make sure your classroom-management structure supports the official rules of the school and aligns with the approaches used by your fellow teachers.

In spite of all of your efforts, you will face some persistent cases of misbehavior. In these cases, don't try to cover up the situation. Rather, consult with veteran teachers for advice, then inform the administration and call the student's home. Parents need to know early on if there are regularly occurring discipline problems with their child. Your call home will be made easier if you have established and maintained open lines of communication with your parent base. Parents will be more likely to support you if you do not limit your calls to behavior problems, but also call with praise for positive student progress. In all cases, maintain meticulous written documentation of parental contacts.

Your own behavior can be the deciding influence in classroom management. Debra G. Gordon remarks,

> As a former general music teacher, I realized that when my students did not perform up to my expectations or they misbehaved, it was ultimately due to my lack of specific directions or insufficient modeling and subsequent rehearsal. I learned this by observing my students in other teachers' classrooms. When I realized that my students' performance, musically and behaviorally speaking, was a direct reflection of my teaching, classroom management and discipline improved immensely.[9]

In all, remember to keep music learning at the center of all classroom routines. After all, making and studying music is what we do throughout our careers. Effective classroom management simply allows us to pursue this journey with a minimum of distraction and wasted time.

Students with Diverse Learning Needs

Part of your regular teaching responsibilities will include working with students who have diverse learning needs. A comprehensive treatment of special education is outside the scope of this book; however, you will find the following information useful as you provide meaningful instruction for these students together with all of your students.

All students have diverse learning needs. If you try to teach your class or ensemble as a faceless mass, you will be spectacularly ineffective because each student requires understanding of his or her personality and learning capabilities. It is now well known that students learn in different ways, and some students require extra attention, or distinct, creative adaptations of your lesson plans and their implementation.

The most important element in instructing students who require special strategies or accommodation is to remember at all times that they are children first and always. Whatever condition they have follows that. So, as some children once were labeled by their condition first and then referred to as children, now, thankfully, educators think first of these students as children. For example, instead of "an autistic child," think of and speak of "a child with autism." The condition is just another part of the learning pathway along which you are leading your students.

Instructional Approaches

Experience and the literature have given us general approaches to instruction that have proven to be effective in this area. "The first step is to find out as much information as one can about individual students."[10] Here, effective communication is of prime importance. What you learn from reading the chapter on communication will help you gather useful information from all of the people who have knowledge about your students' backgrounds and conditions. Along with gathering of information goes collaboration. "Teachers simply cannot meet their growing responsibilities alone. Recent changes in school policies and practices—such as the accountability movement, inclusion, and response to intervention—necessitate that all teachers possess effective communication skills for successfully meeting the needs of a diverse student population."[11] No one expects a single teacher to act in a vacuum to help a student with special needs. To the fullest extent possible, become part of the support team that surrounds the child. This team includes parents or other caregivers, building and district administration, classroom teachers, and the special education staff. Collaborating with this team will enable you to gain valuable information from the child's individual education plan (IEP).

The Individual Education Plan

The IEP is an individualized plan for learning that is tailored to each child's special needs. The IEP will assist you in accommodating the child in your lesson design. If possible, be involved in the development of the child's IEP. If you are unable to do that, in all cases know important elements of the IEP before the child comes to your class or ensemble. This will help you develop appropriate teaching strategies. In the article "Meeting Special Needs in Music Class," Mary S. Adamek suggests creating a "Student Information at a Glance" form that "can provide an overview of the student to aid in instructional development. Typical information includes (1) strengths of the student, along with special skills and talents; (2) weaknesses or limitations of the student; (3) IEP objectives that the student is working on throughout the day; and (4) strategies that are useful when working with this student."[12] Work with the child's support team to complete these thumbnail sketches. Because you have obtained as much information as possible about the child, you can be more confident in effectively meeting needs and designing appropriate instructional adaptations.

Adaptations for Participation

In adapting approaches for participation by special needs students, make sure that the modified lesson activities and experiences are meaningful and respected by the child's peers and do not single out any one student. For example, "A child with a physical disability who is unable to participate meaningfully in a circle dance could be part of a percussion section that provides rhythmic accompaniment for the dance. Other students would also be percussionists, a highly valued musical activity. The rhythmic accompaniment adds to the music experience of the entire class."[13] Students could be rotated through this accompanying percussion ensemble to balance participation. In addition, participation can be meaningfully inclusive in music classes and performing ensembles by adjusting the levels of difficulty according the each child's needs. Balanced, inclusive participation can be achieved by matching an age-appropriate classroom instrument to a child's physical capabilities and skills. For example,

> Even though the student can play the jingle bell easily, it might not be the best choice if the other students are too old to be playing that particular instrument. Whenever possible, make careful instrument choices so that adaptations do not need to be made. For instance, when the rest of the class is playing African percussion instruments, you might offer a light, easy-to-play African basket shaker to a child with limited strength or range of motion.[14]

In a performing ensemble a smaller, lighter version of an instrument could be substituted. For example there are readily available full-range, B-flat trumpets that come in small sizes called "pocket trumpets" that would enable a performer to play all of the music even though limited by arm length or body size. Other band and orchestra instruments come in different sizes as well as different shapes that can be used to meet the needs of certain students. All string instruments are made in a wide variety of sizes, and flutes are now made with curved head joints to match the arm length of performers. Whether in the classroom or performing ensemble, matching instruments to the physical characteristics of each student will go a long way in helping all students succeed.

Modifying Instruction and Grading

Depending on the student, "breaking instruction into smaller steps helps the special learner experience more success."[15] This approach will give you the opportunity to note progress and make changes to ensure steady, even if very slight, advances. You might find that you will have to take even smaller steps with certain children and break down concepts and skills into even smaller segments to achieve progress.

Using improvisation in music classes and ensembles can be an effective means of achieving success for students with diverse learning needs. Through the improvisation experience, students of all abilities can create meaningful music within a nonjudgmental atmosphere. Authentic learning of concepts and skills can take place through this process if structure is provided and clear expectations articulated.

In grading, communicate with the child's support team and link your grades to the goals of the IEP.

> Evaluation and grading should be used to help build positive images. Instruction will need to be adapted and segmented to show continuous progress. While progress may be slower, attainment of each objective should be documented and charted to show progress, so that students and parents will not become discouraged. . . . In some cases, traditional letter grades may be less appropriate than alternative grading systems, such as pass/fail grading, mastery-level grading, or the use of portfolio assessment.[16]

Music Education for All

Overall, it is most important to keep in mind that in public schools *all* students have the right to a music education. The fact that some students have physical or mental conditions that require special attention should not deter you from doing your utmost to give your best to all students. Consistent communication with the support team for children with diverse learning needs is the main ingredient to success in this area. Thoughtful counseling with parents can help students achieve success in the music classroom and provide valuable guidance in selecting a performing group that will hold the most potential for their progress. Soak up all you can in learning special education theory and teaching techniques that now are more and more available in the literature and through such sources as conference presentations and workshops.

In dealing with all students every day, it is well to remember that as a licensed professional in the public service, it is paramount that you keep the worth of each child foremost in your thoughts and actions.

Available resources in special education appear at the end of this chapter. Your best resources, however, will be the special education teacher in your building and your fellow teachers. These front-line teachers will provide you with practical strategies for what works with a variety of students.

Teacher Evaluation

How will your teaching be officially evaluated? Different school districts use different methods, but generally nontenured teachers (often the first three years) are formally observed by the administration more often than tenured teachers. It is common that all teachers will receive written reports based on what an administrator observes when visiting the classroom. Usually at the end of the academic year, you will receive a written evaluation from the administration that might use a format such as the one shown on page 59.

In your preparation for the teaching profession, and as you continue to read and reflect on the areas contained in this book, you would do well to keep the specific areas from this sample evaluation form in mind as a concise checklist of typical expectations. You can use this list of teaching responsibilities, competencies, and relationships as a self-assessment guide for professional growth. You might even want to keep a copy of this sample evaluation form in your plan book as a reminder of your responsibilities.

Planbook Reviews

In addition to classroom observations and the annual evaluation, it is typical that, as a new teacher, your planbook will be reviewed regularly, perhaps weekly, so the administration can verify that you are organized and can put in writing a clear, logical plan of what you intend your students to experience and learn as a result of your lessons. Some districts only require brief synopses of your lessons that you enter into small boxes in your planbook. For these reduced lessons plans, use the items identified with an asterisk in the lesson plan template you entered into your computer. Many districts have a standard lesson plan form that teachers are required to use. If you master the method of lesson planning contained in this chapter, you should be able to adapt your planning to these other lesson plan structures. It is extremely important that you keep in mind that your lesson plans and your classroom observations, in many cases, form the only written record of your teaching, so it is essential that you construct precise, well-structured, and effectively sequenced lesson plans.

Tenure

Upon being recommended by the building and district administration, the Board of Education usually awards tenure to teachers at the end of a

Sample Annual Teacher Evaluation

Baldwin Union Free School District

Baldwin, New York

Annual Teacher Evaluation

TEACHER: SUBJECT/GRADE:

SCHOOL: SCHOOL YEAR:

Rating: S = Satisfactory   NI = Needs Improvement   NE = Not Evaluated

	S	NI	NE
I. Content Knowledge			
A. Exhibits mastery of subject content	—	—	—
B. Keeps up to date in area of specialization	—	—	—
C. Participates in professional development courses/ workshops	—	—	—
D. Implements new strategies	—	—	—
E. Demonstrates professional growth and development	—	—	—
II. Preparation for Instruction			
A. Plans for teaching and learning	—	—	—
B. Provides for individual learning	—	—	—
C. Uses appropriate resources and materials	—	—	—
D. Selects or develops appropriate resources and materials	—	—	—
III. Instructional Delivery			
A. Active student involvement is evident	—	—	—
B. Lesson plans demonstrate meaningful instruction is taking place	—	—	—
C. Uses appropriate teaching techniques	—	—	—
IV. Classroom Management			
A. Maintains approved code of student behavior and discipline	—	—	—
B. Attends to conditions that affect the health and safety of students	—	—	—
C. Establishes and maintains effective classroom routines	—	—	—

(*continued*)

D.   Manages time efficiently   — — —
E.   Organizes the physical environment to facilitate
       instruction   — — —

V.   Student Development
A.   Is sensitive to the needs of students   — — —
B.   Has good rapport with students   — — —
C.   Motivates students and instills a desire to learn   — — —

VI. Student Assessment
A.   Uses the learning standards to measure student
       progress   — — —
B.   Measures student progress on a regular basis using
       multiple assessment techniques   — — —
C.   Adjusts instruction according to outcomes/
       assessments   — — —

VII. Collaboration
A.   Handles reports and written duties efficiently   — — —
B.   Maintains positive school relations   — — —
C.   Communicates effectively with parents   — — —
D.   Contributes to the collective efforts of the department,
       grade, or subject area   — — —
E.   Relates teaching to philosophy and goals of the
       district   — — —

VIII. Reflective and Responsive Practice
A.   Differentiates instruction to meet the needs of diverse
       learners   — — —
B.   Reflects on the aspects of a lesson to refine and
       improve future lessons   — — —

Comments:

_____

Principal   Ass't. Principal   Director/Supervisor   Date

_____

Teacher   Date

_____

**Used by permission of Baldwin public schools.

specified number of years of employment. This can range from three to five years depending on the state or district. Once teachers receive tenure, they can only be removed from their positions for especially egregious issues and problems.

Summary

Effective instruction depends on thoughtful planning that helps students learn how to learn. Effective teachers do not construct plans in their heads as they drive to school each day. To plan effectively you will have to spend a great deal of time reviewing literature and materials, structuring activities, and then plotting out long- and short-range goals. This is all before you even start to write a single daily plan. Planning is important because it serves as a written record of your day-to-day teaching, and provides a clear map of the journey you and your students will take. Careful planning actually saves time because if you decide on the routes you will be taking to your destination, you will know in advance what activities will lead you in the right direction on the journey. Through thoughtful planning, wrong turns can be avoided, and you will not wander around in search of how to satisfy learning standards or the aim of the lesson. However, as with any plan, remember that it is just a plan. It simply lays out what you intend to accomplish. If you get off the track or take a wrong turn, it is not the end of the world. It does not make you a failure. Just take time to think about each lesson and assess what went well and what needs to be changed for future lessons. As you grow in the profession, your lessons will become more and more streamlined, and better connected to the ways each student learns.

It is important to keep in mind that any lesson is only as effective as how it fits into a sequence of learning. You could construct a creative lesson that does not connect with any learning sequence. But this sort of patchwork approach to planning will work against any meaningful learning because the students will not be learning how to learn. Learning how to learn is accomplished, in part, by applying newly acquired knowledge to different situations *within a sequence of content.*

Effective instruction includes understanding how to manage your time and your students. Behavior problems can often be avoided or minimized by a lively lesson pace and the implementation of a well-designed lesson plan. The consistent, fair application of a few rules of behavior will help establish a learning environment that provides clear direction for your students.

Effective instruction includes parents in the learning process. Parents appreciate personal communication that is provided early and often. Consistent connection with your parent base will result in learning that does not stop at the school doors.

The effective delivery of instruction involving students with diverse learning needs will increase your outreach as a teacher as you work to provide all students with their natural right to experience the unique art of music.

In all, your instructional effectiveness will improve as you seek growth in the profession through reflection, reading, research, involvement in professional organizations, and discussion with your colleagues.

In the next chapter, we examine teacher attitude, which is the key that unlocks learning. The command of content you possess and your carefully designed lesson plans will come alive through the way you present material for learning, and how you act and speak with students every day.

For Reflection, Discussion, Assignment

1. Select, or be assigned, one article from the following resources. Provide a review of its main points by using bullets, and explain how you might use what you have learned from the article in your teaching.
2. Write an aim, and construct and discuss two lesson objectives that address that aim. Use a topic of your choosing, or use the following: Fifth-grade class introduction to early jazz—1920s and 1930s. Information about early jazz can be found in the Geoffrey C. Ward book, listed in the Resources section.
3. Using the classroom music lesson plan template from this chapter, construct one lesson plan for elementary classroom music, grade 3, that demonstrates your understanding of the planning process as presented in this chapter. Use the MENC National Standards and accompanying Achievement Standards to select grade-level appropriate concepts and skills for your plan. Access the standards at www.menc.org > Resources > Online Publications > *The National Music Education Standards (The School Music Program: A New Vision)*.
4. Using the sample ensemble rehearsal lesson plan template from this chapter as a guide, construct one ensemble rehearsal plan for grade 8 band, chorus, or orchestra that demonstrates your understanding of the planning process as presented in this chapter. Use the MENC National Standards and accompanying Achievement Standards to select grade-appropriate concepts and skills for your plan. Use two pieces of music in your plan that you have selected through the high-quality literature checklist process from the preceding chapter.
5. Describe how you will use modeling in your teaching.
6. Explain the concept and practice of transfer of knowledge and learning, and describe why and how you will use this transfer in your teaching.
7. Discuss how you will provide reinforcement for the concepts and skills presented in your lessons.

8. Name two ways you will check for individual and group understanding during lesson implementation.
9. Name one technique you will use to provide a class-ending summary to your lessons.
10. Describe the role of parents in the learning process. How will you involve parents in their child's education?
11. Construct a lesson plan using classroom instruments for any elementary grade and provide at least two modifications for students with diverse learning needs.

Resources

Adamek, Mary S. "Meeting Special Needs in Music Class." *Music Educators Journal* 87, no. 4 (January 2001): 23–26.

Adamek, Mary S., and Alice-Ann Darrow. *Music in Special Education.* Silver Spring, MD: American Music Therapy Association, 2005.

Bauer, William I. "Classroom Management for Ensembles." *Music Educators Journal* 87, no. 6 (May 2001): 27–32.

Bernstorf, Elaine D. "Paraprofessionals in Music Settings." *Music Educators Journal* 87, no. 4 (January 2001): 36–48.

Campbell, Patricia Shehan, and Carol Scott Kassner. *Music in Childhood,* 3rd ed. New York: Schirmer, 2009.

Colwell, Richard J., and Michael Hewitt. *Teaching of Instrumental Music,* 4th ed. Upper Saddle River, NJ: Prentice-Hall, 2010.

Conderman, Greg, Sarah Johnston-Rodriquez, Paula Hartman, and Drew Kemp. "What Teachers Should Say and How They Should Say It." *Kappa Delta Pi Record* 46, no. 4 (Summer 2010): 175–81.

Cooper, Lynn G. *Teaching Band and Orchestra: Methods and Materials.* Chicago: GIA, 2004.

Damer, Linda K. "Students with Special Needs." *Music Educators Journal* 87, no. 4 (January 2001): 17–18.

Duke, Robert A. *Intelligent Music Teaching: Essays on the Core Principles of Effective Instruction.* Austin, TX: Learning and Behavior Resources, 2005.

Evertson, Carolyn M., and Edmund T. Emmer. *Classroom Management for Elementary Teachers,* 8th ed. Boston: Allyn & Bacon, 2008.

Gordon, Debra G. "Classroom Management Problems and Solutions." *Music Educators Journal* 88, no. 2 (September 2001): 17–23.

Gumm, Alan. *Music Teaching Style.* Galesville, MD: Meredith Music, 2003.

Hackett, Patricia, and Carolyn A. Lindeman. *The Musical Classroom: Backgrounds, Models, and Skills for Elementary Teaching,* 8th ed. Upper Saddle River, NJ: Prentice Hall, 2010.

Hale, Connie L., and Susan K. Green. "Six Key Principles for Music Assessment." *Music Educators Journal* 95, no. 4 (2009): 27–31.

Haugland, Susan L. *Crowd Control: Classroom Management and Effective Teaching for Chorus, Band and Orchestra.* Lanham, MD: Rowman & Littlefield/MENC: The National Association for Music Education, 2007.

Hourigan, Ryan, and Amy Hourigan. "Teaching Music to Children with Autism: Understandings and Perspectives." *Music Educators Journal* 96, no. 1 (September 2009): 40–45.

Katona, George. *Organizing and Memorizing.* New York: Columbia University Press, 1940.

MENC: The National Association for Music Education. *Spotlight on Making Music with Special Learners: Selected Articles from State MEA Journals.* Lanham, MD: Rowman & Littlefield/MENC, 2004.

Montgomery, Janet, and Amy Martinson. "Partnering with Music Therapists: A Model for Addressing Students' Musical and Extramusical Goals." *Music Educators Journal* 92 (March 2006): 34–39.

Moore, Marvelene C. *Classroom Management in General, Choral, and Instrumental Music Programs.* With Angela L. Batey and David M. Royse. Lanham, MD: Rowman & Littlefield Education, 2002.

Phillips, Kenneth H. *Directing the Choral Music Program.* New York: Oxford University Press, 2004.

Reese, Jill. "The Four Cs of Successful Classroom Management." *Music Educators Journal* 94, no. 1 (September 2007): 24–29.

Regleski, Thomas A. *Teaching General Music in Grades 4–8: A Musicianship Approach.* New York: Oxford University Press, 2004.

Simonsen, Brandi, Sarah Fairbanks, Amy Briesch, Diane Myers, and George Sugai. "Evidence-based Practices in Classroom Management: Considerations for Research to Practice." *Education and Treatment of Children* 31, no. 3 (2008): 351–80.

Snyder, Douglas W. "Classroom Management for Student Teachers." *Music Educators Journal* 84, no. 4 (1998): 37–41.

Sobol, Elise S. *An Attitude and Approach for Teaching Music to Special Learners.* Lanham, MD: Rowman & Littlefield/MENC: The National Association for Music Education, 2008.

Stephensen, Jennifer. "Music Therapy and the Education of Students with Severe Disabilities." *Education and Training in Developmental Disabilities* 41, no. 3 (2006): 290–99.

Ward, Geoffrey C. *Jazz: A History of America's Music.* New York: Alfred A. Knopf, 2000.

Watts, Emily H., and Kimberly McCord. "Collaboration and Access for Our Children: Music Educators and Special Educators Together." *Music Educators Journal* 92 (March 2006): 26–33.

Wong, Harry K., and Rosemary T. Wong. *The First Days of School.* Mountain View, CA: Harry K. Wong, 1998.

Zdzinski, Stephen F. "Instrumental Music for Special Learners." *Music Educators Journal* 87, no. 4 (January 2001): 27–29, 63.

4

The Critical Element: Teacher Attitude

The French philosopher Voltaire said, "The most courageous decision one makes each day is the decision to be in a good mood."[1] Being in a good mood is a great place to start, but the effective music teacher possesses attributes of attitude that go far beyond just mood. Teacher attitude is made up of many parts working together to enable you to use your knowledge of content and methods in communicating effectively with your students.

I served as a central office arts administrator in one school district that each year put on a community event called "In Honor of Excellence." This celebratory meeting featured ten high school seniors chosen by a committee of faculty and administrators. These students then selected and honored three teachers, one each from their elementary, middle, and high school years who had the greatest effect on their lives and learning. The chosen teachers, some of whom had retired while the students were going through their school years, were called to the stage and the seniors spoke about what it was that made these teachers so special in changing their lives. It is worth noting that teachers from the arts were seldom left out of this event. Over several years of observing this occasion and listening to dozens of students speak passionately and often emotionally about their teachers, I can report that without fail the students focused on such attributes of attitude as patience, sense of humor, compassion, enthusiasm, commitment to excellence, and dedication. In many instances the teachers were not even aware of what they had done to cause such monumental changes in the lives of the students. For example, a senior might cite specific encouraging remarks that an elementary teacher had said that had made all the difference in his or her life and studies. Or the students would speak about how certain teachers drew out their best efforts, such as making sure they were called upon and then allowing enough time for them to answer. The specifics of the student recollections about each teacher were stunningly simple, but stand as graphic reminders of the power of what we do and *how* we say what we say in our roles as teachers. It follows that we must take extreme care as we interact with students, because what we do and say can affect students for good or ill for years—perhaps for life. Given the power of teacher attitude in affecting students, it makes sense for you to examine selected areas of attitude, and work to develop an awareness of your own teaching attitudes, and cultivate the ways you interact with students.

Of course, I am sure we would agree that content mastery, knowledge, and skill are essential, but we could also agree that as important as these things are, it is teacher attitude such as noted by these high school seniors that unlocks the door to learning.

Attitude: The *How* of Teaching

In later chapters, you will read of other teachers who have had long-lasting, meaningful effects on their students. If you think about your former teachers who had a positive, enduring effect on your life and learning, you will probably remember *how* they led you to learn rather than *what* specific technical content they focused on. You will most likely remember their teaching effect and their attitude in relation to what you needed at specific times in your development. These teachers demonstrated teaching styles and used strategies that were effective because of aspects of attitude.

Together with command of content and methods, the effective music teacher demonstrates attributes of attitude that connect students with content. In later chapters you will reflect on six components of effective music teaching that align meaningfully with attitudinal teaching traits.

What Makes a Great Teacher?

As was shown in chapter 1, effective teaching has been examined repeatedly through the decades, and the quest continues to find out what effective teachers possess that makes them successful. In the article "What Makes a Great Teacher?" Amanda Ripley notes that since 2002, the federal government's Teach for America program has been gathering data to identify exceptional teachers. As a leader in the Teach for America program, Steven

Farr was tasked with finding out why these exceptional teachers got phenomenal results.[2]

Through multiple classroom observations, lesson plan reviews, and interviews, Farr identified patterns and tendencies common to these outstanding teachers. Ripley reports on Farr's work:

> Right away, certain patterns emerged. First, great teachers tended to set big goals for their students. . . . Great teachers, he concluded, constantly reevaluate what they are doing.
>
> Superstar teachers had four other tendencies in common: they avidly recruited students and their families into the process; they maintained focus, ensuring that everything they did contributed to student learning; they planned exhaustively and purposefully—for the next day or the year ahead—by working backward from the desired outcome; and they worked relentlessly, refusing to surrender to the combined menaces of poverty, bureaucracy, and budgetary shortfalls.[3]

Compare these patterns and tendencies with the results of effective teacher investigations from chapter 1 that have taken place over the years, and you will notice an overwhelming number of traits and characteristics that can be grouped under the heading "Teacher Attitude."

Attributes of Attitude: The ABCs of Attitude

We have examined many traits of effective teaching drawn from the literature that will serve as a foundation for your development. Now consider your own school experiences and think about the attributes of attitude you have observed in the teachers you have had, how they affected you and others, and how you would apply these attitudes to your own teaching. In an ABC format, let's explore these attitudinal areas that include those we've already identified from the research.

As you read each attribute, imagine interacting with students in your music classroom or working with your performing ensemble. Think about how each attribute would be used by you as a key to unlock learning for your students.

ABCs of Attitude

Able, affable: Do you have a friendly, "can-do" approach to your teaching that results in a positive learning environment?

Bold: Is your teaching characterized by confidence in your ability and the success of each student?

Consistent: After clearly articulating expectations, goals, and responsibilities, are you always fair and reasonable in dealing with student response in these areas?

Daring: Do you take risks and try to develop new strategies to help students?

Enthusiastic, Energetic: Are you teacher "DryasDust"? Or "Sour'n'Tired"?

Flexible, Fun: Is your teaching characterized by a willingness to act positively in all situations and with all types of people?

Gracious: Do you maintain a refined and polite demeanor?

Humorous: Does a genuine, natural sense of humor permeate your teaching?

Interested: Are you really committed to the success of each student?

Joyous: Do you exude a positive atmosphere? Are you energized and thrilled about your profession and the possibilities for all students?

Kind: Can you see the good in everyone? Do you really care about each of your students?

Likeable: Are you pleasant and likable, and are you able to see the deep-down likability of your students in spite of their actions?

Motivating: Do you know what each student needs to succeed?

Nurturing: Do students feel your willingness to help, and are they drawn to it?

Organized: Does your teaching demonstrate order and thoughtful planning?

Professional, Passionate, Prepared: Do you maintain the attitude of a licensed professional in all situations? Do you enter each day with passion for your subject along with careful preparation?

Quiet: Do you know when to keep still and really listen to your students?

Rigorous: Are you committed to setting high goals and then providing students with the tools with which to meet or exceed these goals?

Sensitive: Are you tuned in to student needs? Are you so filled with self-importance that you cannot admit to your students and others when you are wrong?

Trustworthy: Do students trust you? (You cannot fake this one!) Do you walk your talk?

Unflappable: How calm in the face of adversity are you?

Valorous: Are you a courageous teacher?

Winsome: How many people are drawn to what you say and do? Do you work on developing a welcoming, winsome teaching demeanor?

Xerophilous: Can you grow where you are planted?

Yielding: Are you willing to yield to what works the best for the good of each student?

Zealous: How much do you care about the success of each student, and how involved with your subject are you?

Able, Affable: Do you have a friendly, "can-do" approach to your teaching that results in a positive learning environment?

It is particularly easy to drag a class or performing group into a downward attitude spiral. It does not take much. For example, ending a classroom session or rehearsal with a tongue lashing accomplishes little more than starting the students on a downward track. Rather, encouraging students with a "you can do this" attitude is much more productive. I once saw a poster on a rehearsal room wall that stated, "Your cooperation is expected and appreciated." That sort of balance between rigor and reasonableness was part of the culture of the students who practiced in that room. The results were emphatically positive and productive.

Bold: Is your teaching characterized by confidence in your ability and the success of each student?

Are you unafraid of expecting the best from your students? Are you forthright in demanding excellence in all areas? I know of one teacher who was bold in setting high goals and demanding excellence; however, he did not provide students with the tools with which to achieve those goals. His ensembles were characterized by performances of music that were beyond the grasp of the group, and the students played without understanding or technical acuity. It was a pity that this teacher did not combine the boldness of high expectations with the means to achieve success. On the other hand, there have been many teachers I have met both in the music classroom and with performing ensembles who have been effective in boldly leading their students to heights of achievement beyond what even the students thought possible.

How did these effective teachers accomplish this? They weren't afraid to forego questionable levels of achievement attained by rote teaching and the use of literature with little merit. Instead, they spent the time necessary to assess the needs and skill levels of their students. Then they crafted a sequence of instruction that set high goals but was linked to appropriate literature and materials. These teachers then provided the guidance necessary for their students to progress steadily to meet and even exceed the goals they were unafraid to set.

Consistent: After clearly and boldly articulating expectations, goals, and responsibilities, and providing your students with the tools with which to succeed, are you always fair and reasonable in dealing with student response in these areas?

Students respect consistency and fairness. It is a deadly practice to create rules, procedures, and consequences and then ignore or, worse, inconsistently enforce them. Students learn very quickly to discount what you say if what you say and what you do are at odds. You can paint yourself into a corner if you put in place unreasonable rules and consequences that you will then have to enforce inconsistently. Better to think long and hard in constructing your structure of class or ensemble expectations. A few well-thought-out rules consistently and fairly applied and enforced will help you manage the learning environment much more effectively than a long list of "do's" and "don'ts."

Consistency and fairness can be quickly established in the classroom or rehearsal if when you give an assignment you follow through and check for compliance. Your credibility in this area will suffer if, for example, you require your students to write a paragraph about selected West African instruments, and then fail to collect the assignment, grade it, and return it with written comments. The same result will occur if you fail to check for compliance at your next orchestra rehearsal after asking the first violins to practice at home from letter A to letter B to produce accurate rhythms, notes, and dynamics.

Before you implement the structure of rules and procedures for your classroom or rehearsal area, it should prove helpful to review your ideas with an experienced teacher. There is no substitute for the wisdom of a veteran, effective front-line teacher. At the very beginning of the school year, or even earlier, make sure students, parents, administrators, and your fellow teachers know what the structure of your classroom or rehearsal environment is and how it will operate. "No surprises!" is a good motto in keeping everyone informed about what to expect with you as the teacher.

Daring: Do you take risks and try to develop new strategies to help all students? Do you work comfortably and enthusiastically with all types of students?

What strategies would you develop and how would you go about teaching students with physical and mental disabilities, or students for whom English is a second language? As you develop lessons to instruct these students, with whom would you work to find out what would be the most effective instructional approaches? What resources would you access to be effective in dealing with such situations? Are you willing to be creatively daring to use a variety of activities and strategies to ensure that all students are learning? To what degree are you daring enough to involve your students' families in the learning process?

Enthusiastic, Energetic: Are you teacher "DryasDust"? Or "Sour'n'Tired"? Do you think your personality is such that someday you might become "burned out"?

I hope it never happens, but this condition could be triggered by any number of things—personal problems at home, unfulfilled aspirations (e.g., unsuccessful as a professional performer), or perhaps "administrivia," such as a large amount of paperwork unconnected to making music.

Think about your energy level. Are you able to sustain your energy and maintain your enthusiasm throughout a long, hard day? It is common that a music teacher's day extends well beyond the stated contract hours for instruction. How well do you maintain an energetic, yet even-keeled, teaching style throughout this type of long day? As important as enthusiasm and energy are, it is important that these attributes of attitude are honest and stem from a genuine passion for your subject and for the development of your students. Fake enthusiasm will be certain to sap your energy and is worse than genuine dourness.

Teachers DryasDust and Sour'n'Tired most likely regularly forget that the study of music and the making of music should be joyous. Yes, there are some aspects of music learning that are not inherently filled with joy, and depend on technical knowledge and study. These aspects include learning note names, rhythm reading, key and meter signatures recognition, scale work, and memorization of songs and other music; however, it is how DryasDust and Sour'n'Tired go about teaching these things that is critically important.

These teachers would benefit from linking every moment of their teaching day to the making of meaningful music. Things might look brighter to these teachers if they have their students at least try to make music in all that they attempt. For example, they could have their students play scales like mini-pieces of music. Note that it is *playing*, not *practicing*, scales. There is a big difference. By playing the scales students are doing two things at once—making music and learning a basic skills vocabulary. If students play their scales with expression and feeling, using dynamic shading and phrasing, the concept of musicality will not be unfamiliar when they play their solos or ensemble pieces. The result might be happier students and happier teachers.

In the general music classroom, DryasDust and Sour'n'Tired might become more effective if they teach their students how to sing songs that connect the music with the meaning of the text by shaping the melody through dynamic contrast, and by choosing which words and syllables to stress for expression.

These teachers might also consider exploring the possibility of teaching at another level, learning another instrument, or joining a community performing ensemble. Attending professional conferences can also help recharge the teaching batteries and alleviate the DryasDust or Sour'n'Tired syndrome.

Flexible, Fun: Is your teaching characterized by a willingness to act positively in all situations, and with all types of people?

You will face students who get under your skin. Some of these students are just not naturally likeable. Throughout your career you will always have some students (or parents, administrators, or even fellow teachers) who somehow know how to push all of your buttons to make you irritable and edgy. How effective will you be with these types of people? How do you plan on meeting these challenges?

In dealing with all types of people, work to overcome snap judgments, sarcasm, and quick, negative retorts. Rather, identify situations in which you are most vulnerable to displays of anger or unreasonableness, and then work to overcome unprofessional conduct in each one. Consider how you will act in the following scenarios: (1) You are being formally observed by the administration as you teach a first-grade class. It starts to snow and the students are overly excited by the sight, and start to get out of control. (2) A fellow teacher is late yet again to pick up her class from the music room while your largest, most active class shows up early. (3) It is the last rehearsal before the concert and your planned rehearsal space is preempted by some other group. (4) Unexpected changes in your rehearsal schedule have been made due to shortened periods, fire drills, or assemblies. (5) You encounter disappointing behavior from your best student (tardiness, alcohol possession on a trip, lack of responsibility, destructive gossip). (6) You are the recipient of negative parent or administrator comments after a concert that you thought went quite well. How well will you deal with these situations?

Start by realizing that you are vulnerable at these times and train your-self to react slowly from the mind rather than emotionally with your mouth. Imagine a gearshift box in your head and when any one of these situations presents itself, take a deep breath, think of the "gearbox," and spend a moment to mentally downshift three or four gears. If you react too quickly by engaging your mouth before your brain is in the appropriate gear, you might say something you may regret later.

Gracious: Do you maintain a refined and polite demeanor? In the face of the situational examples listed previously, how are you going to maintain professional dignity?

Graciousness is not easy to maintain in all situations and with all people. As with the "Flexible, Fun" attribute, you must at times work hard to find your professional dignity. As has been noted, being slow to react is an important component. I have spoken with some teachers who, in times of high stress, have been successful in actively and effectively slowing down their speech and physical movements, and lowering their voice volume. This technique allows the tachometer in your mind to ease out of the red zone, effectively reducing your brain RPMs, which will give you a chance to find that professional demeanor.

You will be better prepared to handle stress if you identify the times you personally feel the most vulnerable before stressful situations actually occur. Here are two more examples from real-life situations. You are on the podium for a final rehearsal before the concert and a fire drill takes place, or at the very last minute your principal asks you to teach a song to your chorus for an unscheduled assembly. Remember to slow down your reactions and draw on your natural sense of humor.

Humorous: Does a genuine, natural sense of humor permeate your teaching?

Effective teaching does not include the use of humor based on sarcasm, but rather finding the humor in situations and human interchange. Experience has shown that student interest levels remain higher and students retain more information for longer periods if humor is used during teaching.

The effective music teacher does not rely on humor that is tacked on (e.g., "Now let's all read the cartoon together and then laugh"). Rather, such a teacher displays humor that is organic, that grows out of and is integrated into what is being studied. Using light-hearted images to obtain better results often helps. For example, you might say, "Amaze your friends and your grandmother in Florida with the words sforzando e stringendo!"

Laughing at yourself is another powerful part of humor in the classroom or rehearsal. We all make mistakes. It is better to own your mistakes and even laugh at them than to get flustered, embarrassed, and angry. Laughing at yourself can go a long way in establishing a positive learning atmosphere.

Interested: Are you really committed to the success of each student?

If you combine this attribute with listening attentively to your students, you will become known as one who is truly interested in students as people. As a result, your students will be much more likely to want to learn in your classes.

I observed one elementary classroom music teacher demonstrate interest and connect with her students through a "News of the Day" feature. At the beginning of each class, one or two students would volunteer to make brief news announcements about something special that they had done during the past week. They made the announcements using a "microphone" created from a paper towel tube the teacher had decorated with sparkles and streamers. The teacher would then sing a short song, inserting lyrics about what the students had announced. As the teacher sang and played for this brief lesson segment, the students performed specific dance moves and clapped rhythms they had learned.

The interest by this teacher in the students' daily lives was effectively connected to making and moving to music. Her students knew she was interested in them individually and personally. Her students responded by making remarkable progress in concept and skills achievement, and in focusing on the week-to-week lesson content.

Joyous: Do you exude a positive atmosphere? Are you energized and thrilled about your profession and the possibilities for all students?

This attitude is not fake joy with a fake smile and fake remarks, but a true spirit of exuberance as you and the students feed off each other and celebrate progress.

Real joy can occur more often than you believe possible if you take the time to establish a connection with your students and together with them connect with the music. This connection model can produce unforgettable moments of joy. The moments need not be rare. These are not once-a-year happenings resulting from complicated situations such as the climax to the high school musical (although there is that joy as well), but simple joys that result from simple pleasures. Examples are when that one fourth-grade boy who can be a handful responds to your encouragement ("You can do this!"), plays all the way through "Ode to Joy" on the recorder, and smiles; or the joy that comes to you and your sixth-grade chorus students because they know that you are working just as hard as they are to learn a piece in another language.

If you interact with your students as a real, genuine, caring person, and together you connect with making and studying music, you will find joy. Don't be surprised by joy. Your positive attitude will produce it.

Kind: Can you see the good in everyone? Do you really care about each of your students?

It might sound terribly trite, but there is power in the age-old Golden Rule, "Do unto others as you would have them do unto you." When students and teachers are asked to identify traits of those teachers who have had a lasting effect on their life and learning, kindness, or some variation of it, appears regularly.

It doesn't matter in which district you teach—there will be students who bring heavy mental or physical baggage to school every day. In poorer districts the students you are asking to sing with feeling might not have had breakfast or have abscessed teeth. In wealthier districts you might have students who are completely isolated from their parents. This "bird in the gilded cage" syndrome occurs when children have everything given to them except the love and companionship of their parents. None of this should cause you to lower your standards or to be overly sentimental, but the knowledge of these realities will help you in connecting with your students. Individual attention to lightening a student's load, even in a small way, should be an integral part of your effective teaching.

Likeable: Are you pleasant and likable, and are you able to see the deep-down likability of your students in spite of their actions?

This attribute extends beyond your own likability, to your ability to find the likability in each of your students. Parents want to hear that you like their child. In spite of things some students do to cause you frustration, you will gain effectiveness in interacting with a wide range of student types and avoid stress if you train yourself to separate the behavior from the child. This is not easy to do; however, if you consistently address the problem, not the person, you could actually end up being able to tell parents that you like their children.

Being able to take the long view with each student also helps in coping with immediate behavior issues. Try giving difficult situations the five-year test. Ask yourself, "If I look back on this situation in five years, how will I view it? How important will it be?" Many times invoking the five-year test will put things in perspective and help you cope with irritating and petty problems, thus giving you more energy and time to deal with more important situations.

Motivating: Do you know what each student needs to succeed?

Almost all students welcome and function better in a structured learning environment. Students need to know exactly what is expected of them, how to practice and study to meet these expectations, and how they are going to be evaluated on their achievement. Some students need an extremely directed, structured, step-by-step process laid out for them in order to achieve success. However, there are those students who will bridle at this, not produce good work, and rebel while characterizing this approach as heavy handed and overly restrictive. These students could thrive under a lighter teacher touch, with you helping them set their own goals and working with them to develop ways to achieve those goals. In this case you act as more of a coach and cheerleader as the students move toward achieving the goals they have set and have ownership of. It is up to you to find out what buttons to push to get each student to learn. Teaching is definitely not a "one size fits all" profession.

Nurturing: Do students feel your willingness to help, and are they drawn to it?

This attitude is not the treacly, sentimental type of approach that sugarcoats real problems that must be faced and dealt with. There are some teachers who praise students even when they do not earn the praise. This approach creates conflict between what the students know to be true and what these teachers insist on saying. The result is that the students often dismiss *everything* said by these teachers because the praise has been so devalued.

Demonstrate a nurturing attitude by providing students with the tools necessary to achieve success. You might become frustrated because some of the tools you provide are not used or don't seem to work with certain students. The key is to not give up. If one approach or tool does not work, use another. Eventually, even if multiple tools result in only modest gains in achievement, students will at least understand and appreciate the fact that you are spending time with them in a sincere effort to help them succeed. Avoid the "everything is beautiful" attitude that lavishes praise when it is not warranted. Add value to your praise by encouraging students to earn it.

In the article "What Makes a Great Teacher?" cited previously, the admissions staff of Teach for America examined data relative to predictors of success. The one trait that stood out "was a history of perseverance—not just an attitude, but a track record. In the interview process, Teach for America now asks applicants to talk about overcoming challenges in their lives—and ranks perseverance based on their answers."[4] Draw on challenges you have overcome in your own life and persevere in your nurturing.

Organized: Does your teaching demonstrate order and thoughtful planning?

By being organized you will provide your students and yourself with a clearly delineated pathway to travel toward success. It is much easier to lead if you know where you are headed. Goal setting and planning the objectives to meet these goals is a skill that can be learned. Recall the lesson plan models that appear in chapter 3. These models provide a useful organizational framework for your instruction. Daily planning can be extended to produce a successful, long-range learning pathway that includes multiple lessons. Even longer-range goals can benefit from your grasp of effective daily planning. An example is the sequence of instructional units that covers the five years of K–4 in music reading, singing, and improvisation. Assessment and achievement both depend on your thoughtful, sequential planning, and attention to detailed organization.

In developing your organizational skills, "know thyself." For example, I observed a music teacher over the course of several years who did not possess many gifts in the area of organization, but she realized that fact and made it her business to spend the time and energy necessary to become organized. She had to take more time than other teachers in planning and organizing, but she did it because she knew that with effective organization her program would be more likely to flourish.

A warning about organization and planning is necessary. Despite all of your careful planning, goal setting, and structuring, there will always be unforeseen obstacles and elements of surprise. Things will happen. It is important that you do not let changes in your well-thought-out planning throw you for a loop. Stay calm and professional. For example, early in the day I carefully set up my orchestra for an evening concert only to return and find many of the chairs had been taken for an unscheduled event in another part of the building. Thankfully, I had arrived in plenty of time before the concert so I was able to work alongside the custodians to find other chairs and reset the ensemble. Always prepare for the worst and hope for the best. Think about your organizational skills, be honest in assessing your potential for success or failure, and work to grow in this critically important area.

Professional, Passionate, Prepared: Do you maintain the attitude of a licensed professional in all situations? Do you enter each day with passion for your subject along with careful preparation?

There is a professional demeanor that can be cultivated and become useful in managing the learning environment, meeting with parents, and interacting with administrators, fellow teachers, and community members. Consider the demeanor of other licensed professionals such as physicians. The way they dress, speak, and conduct themselves usually removes any doubt as to their position and command of their knowledge area. Of course, some professionals overplay their role so you should not emulate those behaviors, but your demeanor, including the way you speak, dress, and are groomed, can go a long way in establishing you as the positive leader.

As a passionate professional, you will exude a deep involvement with your subject combined with an unrelenting commitment to seeing your students enjoy what the art of music offers. The results of your teaching passion can be remarkable. Students often will try something new or attempt to succeed just because you exhibit your utter love for all aspects of music together with their success in learning. Your passion can kick-start their involvement that then can deepen and grow as a result of your artistry and attitude.

The passionate, prepared professional forms a powerful package of effective teaching. Combine your love and knowledge of subject matter with careful preparation, act as the licensed professional you are, and unlock learning with each student through your attributes of attitude.

Quiet: Do you know when to keep still and really listen to your students? Do you let your energy and enthusiasm get in the way of taking the time to wait for students' responses? Do you take the time to listen intently for subtexts of what students are trying to or need tell you?

Part of being quiet is making the time to deal with students one on one. It can be extremely informative and helpful if you speak with some students individually. This technique can be useful with students who are disruptive or who have other problems in acting appropriately in the classroom or rehearsal. By calmly and quietly listening to what they have to say without the distraction of peers, you might find out information that will assist you in helping them to achieve success.

Be careful, however, that in interacting with students one on one you make sure to follow your district's policies and procedures. This is particularly important in the case of Internet social networks, texting, and e-mail. Any contact with students via social networks could be misconstrued and might expose you unnecessarily to accusations of impropriety. Texting and e-mail messages can be misinterpreted or carry an unintended tone. Be extremely careful in using these types of communication. As a licensed professional you must be careful to maintain a distinct line between teacher and student. A good practice to follow is to keep your private life private, but always make the time to really listen to your students.

Rigorous: Are you committed to setting high goals and then providing students with the tools with which to meet or exceed these goals?

So many of the attributes of teacher attitude center on matters of caring, compassion, nurturing, and the like that it is easy to forget that rigorous achievement expectations go hand in hand with supportive attributes. Students will achieve more if you set attainable, high goals and then persevere in leading them to meet them. To do this, you must first know where the starting achievement levels of your students are. Once you have established those levels you can set the bar as high as you think they can attain. This really is the core of teaching and is easier said than done. However, students will achieve higher success if you set high standards. On the other hand, setting very low goals will cause high-achieving students to lose interest and will actually hold back those students with modest abilities. Continuously monitor student progress to find the appropriate balance between these two approaches.

Sensitive: Are you tuned in to student needs? Are you so filled with self-importance that you cannot admit to your students and others when you are wrong?

This sort of sensitivity is not the type that causes you to feel hurt when students act out, but rather it is an awareness of the complicated patchwork of needs your students possess. Work to find out about what makes each of your students tick and use that information to help them learn and succeed.

Trustworthy: Do students trust you? (You cannot fake this one!) Do you walk your talk?

Our actions really do speak louder than our words. You must be very careful in what you say because your students are experts in connecting what you say with what you do. One disconnect might not hinder your trustworthiness, but if you exhibit a pattern of saying one thing and doing another, your students will tune you out.

Unflappable: How calm in the face of adversity are you?

Are you able to recognize and deal effectively with potentially volatile situations involving students, parents, other teachers and administrators? This attribute is not unlike preparing for a college examination. If you have studied regularly, prepared scrupulously, and dedicated yourself to the success of each student, then you can be confident and unflappable as you walk into the classroom. However, the real test of your unflappability will be how you react to unexpected situations. I observed a kindergarten class during which one child became ill during a song the group was singing. The veteran teacher didn't become fazed at all. She wisely and quickly gathered the class at the front of the room and kept the class singing while she went to the door to call the hall monitor for assistance. She certainly demonstrated a useful, unflappable demeanor.

Valorous: Are you a courageous teacher?

Are you brave enough to keep trying different approaches even when every one of your efforts has not produced a positive result? Do you have the courage to stand up to unreasonable and prickly, picky parents, fellow teachers, and administrators by offering, as diplomatically as possible, specific and compelling reasons for why music must be a necessary part of every child's education? Are you valorous enough to be an advocate for your students' success?

Winsome: How many people are drawn to what you say and do? Do you work on developing a welcoming, winsome teaching demeanor?

Part of developing an effective teaching demeanor is working on your winsomeness. If pomposity and condescension are elements of demeanor to be avoided, winsomeness is one to be sought and used. Ask yourself, "Would I want to be a student in my classroom?" Be the kind of teacher that students want to learn from. I know one teacher who has a naturally restrained, dry sense of humor and a soft voice. She is successful in winning students' hearts and minds by using this soft but insistent voice and this special brand of humor. Winning ways cannot be produced via a formula, however. You must find and fit your winsomeness into your natural personality. The goal is to win the students with your natural interest in them—who they are, what they do, what they think.

Xerophilous: "Thriving in a hot, dry climate."[5] Can you grow where you are planted?

Will you flourish even when you are not nourished? Or are you a bottomless pit of wants and needs that seem to hinder your teaching at every turn? Strive to look for opportunity where others might see obstacles. I taught middle school band sectionals for some time in the front lobby of a school. Rather than whine about the situation and refuse to go on, I was happy that my program was so large that my teaching schedule had to include alternate areas for rehearsal. Plus, my program was always front and center for all to see and hear every day, especially when I had a percussion sectional!

A teacher inherited an elementary string program that had all but evaporated. Instead of giving up, this teacher tripled the size of participation by increasing communication with parents and involving a great many students in small ensembles that played at every conceivable event—PTA meetings, senior centers, nursing homes, and school art shows. Growing where she was planted, this teacher used these approaches together with a genuine passion and enthusiasm for making music with children. The result was a blockbuster string program.

Yielding: Are you willing to yield to what works the best for the good of each student?

Are you willing to put aside your ego and pride for the good of individual student growth? Sad to say that teacher ego gets in the way of much student progress. We have all heard performing ensembles attempt music that is simply too hard for the students. One has to wonder if the director is performing this advanced literature just to feed his or her ego. "Well, my group only performs level 6 literature" might translate into "My ego demands that I will not be seen conducting a group performing any literature lower than level 6." Better to have the attitude that the important thing is to select performance literature of a level that fits the achievement level of your students, is of high quality, and develops musical concepts and skills.

Zealous: How much do you care about the success of each student, and how involved with your subject are you?

Zealotry should not be confused with an overbearing, crazed fanaticism, but rather should be viewed as a passionate commitment to the goals of the profession. You should be so zealous that you will find yourself giving of yourself again and again to help all students become all they are capable of becoming. Music teachers who give of themselves to this degree can be assured that somewhere down the line, a student or two or one hundred will carry into the future a fulfillment that cannot be put into words, but which will remain a priceless product of your teaching. That is what makes what we do worthwhile.

In a later chapter you will read of teachers who personify each one of the ABCs of attitude, and who have had a lasting influence for good with students who have gone on to continue the legacy.

Summary

In all, teacher attitude is at the heart of all teaching and learning. You can be a virtuoso musician with blazing technique, perfect pitch, and deep theoretical and historical knowledge; however, if you are unable to cause students of widely varying backgrounds, abilities, and attitudes to achieve success, all of this talent will not be of much use in the learning process. On the other hand, if you have extraordinary attitudinal skills and you do not possess command of subject matter and technical acuity, you will be limited in how far you will be able to lead your students. If you are only keeping one or two lessons ahead of your students, it is questionable to what degree your students will be able to develop. The combination of command of subject and effective teaching attitude is critically important to student growth. At all times you must keep in mind that you are dealing with individual students who possess unique personalities and who require nuanced teaching approaches tailored to their needs. Developing positive attributes of attitude will help you lead your students to realize potential that perhaps even they did not know they possessed.

The Power of Your Attitude

Haim Ginott movingly sums up attitude and effective teaching.

> I have come to a frightening conclusion. I am the decisive element in the classroom. It is my personal approach that creates the climate. It is my daily mood that makes the weather. As a teacher I possess tremendous power to make a child's life miserable or joyous. I can be a tool of torture or an instrument of inspiration. I can humiliate or humor, hurt or heal. In all situations it is my response that decides whether a crisis will be escalated or de-escalated, and a child humanized or de-humanized.[6]

In the next chapter, artistry and attitude come together and are applied to all aspects of the school community through the means of effective communication, which is one of six components of effective music teaching to which you will be introduced.

For Reflection, Discussion, Assignment

1. Reflect on how your teaching affect and approaches will align with the ABCs of attitude, and provide for each attitude one example of how you might apply it to your teaching.
2. Reflect on and discuss attitudes exhibited by teachers you have had from the past. How were you affected by these attitudes? If you had been the teacher, what would you have done differently to cause more effective learning?
3. Name and discuss attitudinal challenges and solutions that could be part of the bulleted situations below. For each situation, do the following:

a. Identify possible areas or issues of concern and opportunities for success.
b. Review the ABCs of attitude in this chapter, and identify the attitudes that would help address those areas of concern and opportunities for success you have identified.
c. Be prepared to discuss how you would apply the attributes of attitude you have selected to these areas or issues of concern and opportunities for success.
   - Field trips
   - Ensemble performance trips
   - Ensemble competitions
   - Solo competitions
   - Fundraising projects
   - Booster club relations: your relations with the booster club, student relations with the booster club, booster club members' relationships among themselves
   - Auditioning students for seat placement or solos
   - Auditioning students for solos or parts in a musical
   - Choosing students for leadership roles (e.g., section leaders, drum major, ensemble officers, classroom project leaders)
   - Choosing students for awards
   - Choice of performance literature
   - Classroom or rehearsal management
   - Conquering technical and musical challenges in the performance literature
   - Encouraging creativity and musicality
   - Communication with students, parents, fellow teachers, administrators, community leaders and groups

Resources

Farr, Steven. *Teaching as Leadership: The Highly Effective Teacher's Guide to Closing the Achievement Gap.* Hoboken, NJ: John Wiley and Sons, 2010.

Ginott, Haim G. *Teacher and Child: A Book for Parents and Teachers.* New York: Macmillan, 1972.

Lautzenheiser, Tim. *The Art of Successful Teaching: A Blend of Content and Context.* Chicago: GIA, 1992.

———. *The Joy of Inspired Teaching.* Chicago: GIA, 1993.

Lemov, Doug. *Teach Like a Champion: 49 Techniques that Put Students on the Path to College.* Hoboken, NJ: John Wiley and Sons, 2010.

Sonntag, Steven. *Teaching, the Hardest Job You'll Ever Love: Helpful Ideas for Teachers In and Out of the Classroom.* Lanham, MD: Rowman & Littlefield Education, 2010.

Whitaker, Todd. *What Great Teachers Do Differently: 14 Things That Matter Most.* Larchmont, NY: Eye on Education, 2003.

5

Effective Communication and Six Components of Effective Teaching: Artistry and Attitude Together

This chapter focuses on effectively communicating and connecting with your students, other students, parents, administrators, the community, fellow teachers, and staff. You will also be introduced to six components of effective teaching that are aligned with descriptive traits derived from the research literature and what you know is true from the effective teachers you have had.

Effective Communication

The effective music teacher is an effective communicator. You will face an uphill struggle in leading students to learn if you do not actively work on developing strong communication skills that connect you not only with your students but also with all parts of the network that surrounds them. Who are the people that form this network? Certainly your own students, but you must include the other students in the school because they most assuredly contribute to the network. You must also consider parents, fellow teachers and staff, administrators, and the community. This network also includes society in general and the culture each student comes from.

All of these components interconnect and influence your students to a degree that demands consistent and regular communication. Improved relations with these constituent groups can have a positive effect on student learning. For example, make sure to connect with community members who do not have children in the music program. They might not understand the need for funds to provide the latest materials or to pay for field trips that provide program enrichment. They also might not be aware of music study that is available for them through evening course offerings at your school. It might have been some time since they were in school, so it will be helpful to keep them up to date as part of your effort to surround your students with an informed constituency.

What can you expect as a result of your effective communication? The benefits are many and include the following:

- Positive learning environment. *(If students and parents find that they can dialogue freely with you, the result will be an encouraging atmosphere conducive to progress.)*
- Assessment of student progress. *(Students and parents who are kept informed about progress early and often are provided with the opportunity to address areas in need of improvement before it is too late.)*
- Additional strategies for student achievement growth. *(Teachers, students, and parents can develop alternate learning strategies to improve achievement levels if the lines of communication among all constituents are kept active.)*
- Multiple pathways for discipline and management. *(Issues of behavior that hinder individual learning can be addressed efficiently and effectively if you work to maintain a regular dialogue with your students and parents. A variety of ways to address behavior difficulties can be developed and applied if you consistently communicate with administrators, fellow teachers, and parents.)*
- Trust and respect. *(By communicating honestly and freely with your students, you will soon gain the reputation of one who really cares about them as humans. As you exhibit honesty and fairness in your daily contact with students, you will gain their trust and respect. Caring, trust, and respect are three essential elements that will help form a productive relationship with students and their support network.)*
- Understanding. *(You will understand your students more fully if you maintain an open pathway of communication with them based on positive attributes of attitude that you develop.)*
- Support and advocacy for your program. *(Through effective communication, all constituents surrounding your program will grow. You will enjoy increased support for your program by keeping all parts of the surrounding community informed and involved.)*

Communicate by Connecting

What are some ways to develop your communication skills? Remember the ABCs of attitude in chapter 4? You will recall that every single one of these attributes can be directly applied to building effective communication skills. Use these ABCs of attitude to create productive communication connections with all parts of the learning network.

Using the ABCs of attitude as a foundation, think about how to communicate with three important constituencies. Communicate by connecting with (1) the life of the building, district, and community; (2) the lives of your students' parents; and (3) the lives and learning of your students. By connecting with these three groups you will build a support system that can have a dramatic, positive effect on all students.

Connect with the Life of the Building, District, and Community

Find out what the mission, goals, and ideals of your building, district, and community are and see how you can address them effectively through your program. Each school district has written statements that articulate these areas, and each community will exhibit a character or profile based on commonly held traditions and values. Align your program with these constituents through the choice of appropriate high-quality literature. Community members are well aware of the words their children are singing and the types of music they are studying and performing. Be sensitive and work to complement the character of the community. Learn about your community by attending Board of Education meetings, joining the parent-teacher association (PTA), becoming involved in a service or social group, or by being part of a local house of worship. Provide music for PTA functions, Board of Education meetings, school awards nights, and local nursing homes.

Community members such as senior citizens who don't have children in school will benefit from learning more about music and be more likely to support the music program if they attend your concerts, musical productions, and field shows. So why not build productive connections by inviting them to visit your classroom or attend your performances? You might want to provide a "What to Listen For" handout as part of every printed concert program. This practice will result in a more knowledgeable and supportive audience. Also, to further enhance connections with this group, don't hesitate to have your students perform at the local senior center.

Connect and communicate with the building and district administration by keeping them informed at all times. An informed administrator is a happier administrator. As a matter of practice, you should know and abide by all school policies even when you are tempted to bend the rules. For example, if the policy of the district is that the high school marching band must be off the field at a certain time, make sure to respect and follow the requirement. If you start bending rules, the students will be sure to notice and question your integrity. By skirting school procedures you could end up placing your fellow teachers and the administration in uncomfortable situations. Keep the administration up to date on your successes and don't attempt to hide your mistakes. It is always a good practice to show your administrator any written communication you intend to send home. You don't want your administrator to be surprised to learn from a parent about something that you have done or intend to do. The administrator should hear it from you first.

To create a special connection, try involving your administrator in your program. One orchestra teacher had her building principal play the triangle on a piece. The principal was determined to get her part right but rehearsal time ran out and the concert was the next evening, so the principal scheduled an extra rehearsal! At the concert, the principal performed well and also became more attuned to the extensive preparation needed to perform, as well as the value of rehearsal time. Another teacher had her principal come to music class and participate in a music and movement lesson.

Administrator involvement can even breed traditions. As an example of a comprehensive connection with constituents, I know of a large high school that has a long-standing tradition of the entire administration, students, alumni, parents, community members, and teachers all singing the various parts of a well-known Christmas piece at the annual holiday concert. I am certain you will discover your own ways to connect with your learning and support network.

As a new teacher you will be overwhelmed with a variety of demands. Paperwork, meetings, lesson planning, and a host of other responsibilities will consume large amounts of time, but it is vitally important to make the time to connect with fellow teachers from other departments through socialization. Teachers from all departments are dedicated, but it seems that music teachers are always meeting with students long before and after school for rehearsals, as well as working with students at lunchtime, and organizing fundraising activities and field trips. This is only the tip of the iceberg when it comes to being an active music teacher. Even so, do whatever it takes to interact with faculty. Have lunch with them. After school hours, attend faculty social events. Join the faculty sports team. Volunteer to chaperone and be involved personally in school and community events such as dances, sports contests, assemblies, charity events, and activities run by fellow teachers. Above all, connect and communicate with the building staff including the custodians. Make sure you greet them regularly with a smile and a kind word. Their jobs often are repetitive and thankless, but without their expertise, the school could not function. Find out when their birthdays are, send a card, and bring goodies for the front office counter. Become a contributing part of the life and health of your building, district, and community.

Because you are involved with this constituency on a social level, professional interaction will flow more naturally. For example, if you want to put together an interdisciplinary world culture night involving several departments, you will find the planning and implementation of such a project much easier if you have established a social connection with the other teachers. You will save time and enjoy designing the event because you will be able to discuss particulars regularly and informally as part of your natural interaction. You might not even need any formal meetings to organize this interdisciplinary initiative. If you are effectively connected to the community, you might be able to involve participants such as ethnic bands and dancers from the surrounding area to enhance this special event.

Connect with the Lives of Your Students' Parents

Work to reach out to parents who are not actively involved in your program. Don't depend on Back to School Night. The parents who attend that event are almost always the involved parents. You will soon discover who the active parents are. Communication and involvement can improve by pairing these active parents with inactive parents. But the parent pairs need a specific duty or project on which to focus. Parents can bond quickly by working together this way for a common goal, even if it is something quite simple such as a one-day car wash fundraiser. If you are active alongside the parents and students with such projects, it will provide you with an informal avenue for communication. You can establish good relations and learn a lot about the way your parents and students think while you are scrubbing wheel rims at the chorus car wash. In turn, parents and students will appreciate your willingness to roll up your sleeves and pitch in.

In the chapter on effective instruction, you learned to communicate with parents what you are grading, how you are grading, what your grades mean, and what students should do to receive the best grade possible. One band director I know placed a large poster on the wall with a heading that read, "How to get an A+ in band." Below, she listed specific requirements to earn an A+ and what the lower grades meant. She also placed this information in the student handbook and in the welcome letter to parents at the start of school. There was no question in anybody's mind how to achieve an A+ in that class. Another teacher regularly called parents with messages of praise for specific achievements and marked progress. He also called with warnings about lack of progress or behavior issues. By keeping the lines of communication open through this personal touch, his program grew in size and quality.

An especially effective way to communicate and connect with parents is to create opportunities for them to be involved in learning content along with their children. Examples of how to engage parents in this powerful pathway for communication are provided later in this chapter. Communicating with parents and students from other cultures can also be improved by using this process.

Connect with the Lives of Your Students

Keep in mind that your students have lives outside of music class, so go cheer for your students and their friends at their athletic contests. You will not believe the positive effect that will have on your relationship with your students and their parents. Jaws will drop when you are spotted on the sidelines yelling encouragement. Offer to chaperone dances and field trips. Learn and use the names of all music students and other students at your school. Remember your students' birthdays. Seek opportunities to become involved with students from other departments and other areas of the music department. Be the teacher who judges the Sports Night competition or who accompanies the science club on a trip to gather specimens. Reach out to other grade levels and parts of the music program. If you are a high school band director, why not on occasion volunteer to run a rehearsal at the elementary level? After all, you will be inheriting these students in a few years and your visit will help strengthen the idea that ensemble participation is a multiyear sequence. Or, as an orchestra director, help your fellow music teachers and custodians set up the chorus risers. As an elementary classroom music teacher, interact with performing ensembles by having older students demonstrate the instruments to enhance a unit of study on the instruments of the orchestra.

Communicate through Committee Service

There will be plenty of opportunity for you to get involved with building and district committees. Your available time will be limited, but consider providing some committee service, especially if the committee is engaged in curriculum or staff development, scheduling, or other areas that could affect the music program. A voice from the music area on these committees can be invaluable, as it will allow you to provide information and direction to the deliberations before decisions are made that are difficult to reverse. For example, one high school entered into a faculty committee discussion dealing with master schedule redesign. As a committee member, the music teacher was able to point out alternatives to a schedule that would have broken the multiyear sequence of the band program. The plan that was being considered would have prevented particular instrumentalists from participating for various semesters. She would have lost her entire double reed section for the spring concert season if she had not served on that committee and provided that information. But don't serve on committees simply to protect the music program. I would hope you would serve because you really want to be involved in the entire life and health of all aspects of the building and district. Caring for the educational progress of students outside of the music area should be part of your attitudinal essence as an effective music teacher.

Communicate through Sharing Goals

Building shared goals among music teachers across the district and within each building can be an effective means of increasing communication. Districtwide goals are usually worked out as part of large scale initiatives that stem from state and regional accrediting agencies together with standards of learning requirements from state departments of education. You can support these broad district goals and improve communication by working cooperatively at the building level to create a unified music department. If you are the only music teacher in your building, it will take a little more effort, but the students will benefit if you team up with music teachers from other buildings, or if you simply coordinate the goals of your music program with other nonmusic faculty in your building. It is the shared-goals aspect that is important to understand and implement. This coordinated approach helps the learning process because students will receive reinforcement in concepts and skills no matter what group or no matter which teacher they happen to have. Your program will also function more efficiently if there are structural and procedural expectations common to all parts of the department. Through this consistency students will quickly learn the culture of the department: "This is what we do here" and "That is not what we do here."

As a new teacher you might hesitate to initiate such a shared-goals process; however, it really is not complicated or time consuming. It simply means getting together with your fellow teachers to make sure you all are on the same page in a few important areas. This is essential because as the new teacher it will help you to know what the common expectations are. Getting together will provide the opportunity to discuss previous goals and make adjustments, if necessary. Before the school year begins, get together with your colleagues and agree on a short list of goals that could be applied to all parts of the program. You might also want to agree on ways to assess student achievement for these goals. For example, you might agree that all students in all performing groups will attempt to excel in the following areas: (1) responsibility, (2) tone quality, (3) intonation, and (4) accuracy of basic skills (notes, rhythms, dynamics, blend, balance, phrasing, and ensemble precision).[1] The value of this exercise is that no matter what ensemble they are in, the students will clearly know department expectations. The students in special groups such as marching band, jazz band, jazz choir, and the musical production should not be overlooked in this process.

Another way to build shared goals includes working collegially on program planning that takes into account the master schedule for your building, and other commitments and demands on your students' time.

Communication Attitude

All of these ideas sound great, but where will you get the time to do all of it? The answer is that you won't have time to do all of it, just some of it. Your attitude toward connecting with the constituents that form your learning network is the most important component. If you have a willing, cooperative attitude, you will find the time to engage in some of the interaction suggested in this chapter that will result in a constituent culture of cooperation and communication. Surely learning will have a better chance to succeed within this caring, supportive atmosphere.

Communicate Nonverbally

In addition to using the approaches discussed previously to communicate and connect with your students and their constituent network, work to develop nonverbal communication techniques in the classroom or rehearsal hall. The chapter on effective instruction contains nonverbal strategies to aid in classroom management and to help you save time through establishing routines and structure. Here we examine additional ways to increase teaching effectiveness through nonverbal communication that will affect students' perceptions about what you are saying.

Sharyn L. Battersby, in the article "Increasing Awareness in the General Music Classroom," asks, "How are we communicating to our students, and how do they really see us?" and "Do we recognize our students' nonverbal behaviors as response indicators to our lessons?"[2] William J. Seiler and Melissa L. Beall, in *Communication: Making Connections*, state that "we are always communicating something nonverbally, whether we intend to or not. Besides occurring constantly, nonverbal communication depends on context, is more believable than verbal communication, is a primary means of expression, is related to culture, and is ambiguous or easily misunderstood."[3]

Messages students receive from you will be influenced by your facial and eye expressions, body language, and tone and volume of voice. Likewise, student response to instruction will be indicated by these three areas. Confusing communication can occur if what you are saying is conveyed in a contradictory manner by nonverbal means. On the other hand, if what you are saying is supported by your nonverbal communication, the message will be less ambiguous and have a more lasting effect.[4]

Try this exercise. Use a monotone to state, "Over the weekend I am going to review Professor Smith's lecture on planning, and write lessons for my kindergarten classes." Now restate the sentence, still in a monotone, but use subtle facial and eye expressions to either support or contradict the meaning of the sentence. If you simply roll your eyes just a little bit while you say "Professor Smith's lecture," you would certainly convey a special message about Professor Smith and his lectures. If you make a grimace when you say "kindergarten classes," you would send a negative message about your kindergarten classes.[5]

Repeat the sentence and use body language to either reinforce or contradict what message you are sending. For example, choose a part of the sentence that you view negatively, and as you say it, fold your arms tightly across your chest and turn your head away. This will reveal what you really mean in what you are saying. Repeat the sentence and vary the message by emphasizing different words and using a variety of tone and volume in your voice to convey various meanings to what you will be doing over the weekend. The exercise can be repeated using combinations of eye and facial expression, body language, and vocal tone and volume.

This simple exercise demonstrates how what you say can produce either clear or confusing messages, and can positively or negatively influence the learning atmosphere in your classroom. Be aware that your students will also send messages through nonverbal means. You will be able to understand their responses more fully if you pay close attention to the match between their verbal and nonverbal communication.

Communication and Culture

Cultural consideration also plays an important part in communicating effectively with students from all backgrounds. For example, in the United States, making and maintaining eye contact with students can often enhance communication and learning, but in some cultures where the sexes do not generally interact, eye contact can be interpreted as being rude or overly familiar. Misunderstanding can occur in teaching students from such cultures. Awareness of cultural differences can help improve your communication with a diverse student body.

Communication Distractions

Verbal and physical "tics" can change or distract from the message meaning. The overuse of "like," "you know," "I mean," or "um" can result in a weaker message, reduced student confidence in teacher competency, and reduced focus on the content of the message. Physical "tics" might include favoring one side of the class by consistently teaching to the students on your right or left. Other such tics include head scratching, hand wringing, and gestures and movements not connected to the message you are trying to convey. All of these can distract from clear communication. In ensemble conducting, try to have every movement express something. Gestures not connected to the musical message of the piece will detract from its meaning.

The Power of Nonverbal Communication

Nonverbal communication is a potent part of connecting with your students during instruction but is an equally powerful agent as you connect with parents, administrators, fellow teachers, and the community at large.

The area of nonverbal communication is complex; however, awareness of its constant presence and power will help you use it to create a positive learning environment, and will help you understand responses from your students more completely. Activities for your improvement in this area appear at the end of this chapter.

Communicate through Parental Collaboration

What follows is a particularly effective way to communicate with parents and students, and improve relationships between the school and home. The Connecting Parents with Learning Project (CPLP) combines artistry and attitude in special ways. It artfully combines content, method, and attitude by engaging students and parents cooperatively learning content together. The process of implementing a CPLP is described in the following section, and sample projects and materials are provided. Use the sample ideas or develop your own project. The CPLP represents communication in action.

Implement a "Connecting Parents with Learning Project" in Your School[6]

According to the U.S. Department of Education, "Education research over the past three decades has established a direct correlation between increased parent involvement and increased student achievement."[7] Diana Hiatt-Michael writes,

> A review of research over the past two decades confirms the importance of parent involvement. Teachers' efforts to involve families promote the following: better student attendance; higher graduation rate from high school; fewer retentions in the same grade; increased levels of parent and student satisfaction with school; more accurate diagnosis of students for educational placement in classes; reduced number of negative behavior reports; and, most notably, higher achievement scores on reading and math tests.[8]

The benefits of parental involvement are obvious, but it is important to take a look at *how* we involve our parents. Most likely the parents of our students really want to be involved but often don't know how to get involved beyond volunteer efforts. Do we as music educators know how to involve our parents in the learning process?

The fact is that we do a pretty good job at keeping parents informed *about* our programs and involving parents through volunteer efforts such as booster clubs. As valuable as these efforts are, why not seek ways to go beyond public relations and try a teaching approach that involves parents in actively learning content along with their children?

What is the Connecting Parents with Learning Project?

The CPLP is an attempt to involve parents in learning standards-based content along with their children. The CPLP can be especially effective in connecting with parents of different cultures because the children teach the parents. Furthermore, it removes the mystery of what the students are studying by engaging parents and students in cooperative learning and by presenting content in manageable portions. The CPLP is particularly effective if it is based on local and national standards for music learning, and if it is integrated with learning in other subject areas.

The purposes of the CPLP are (1) to strengthen parent-student-school relations, (2) to increase content knowledge, and (3) to improve music listening and performance skills.

The CPLP involves parents in learning what their children are studying through the use of teacher-prepared materials. Parents interact with material sent home and are quizzed by their own children on the content. Parents reciprocate by quizzing their children on similar content. Upon completion of the project, parents, students, and the teacher complete surveys that assess the effectiveness of the project and offer suggestions for changes. Performing group and classroom teachers at all levels can use this approach to involve parents. As an additional benefit, parent advocacy can be strengthened if parents are significantly involved with the music program by learning together with their children.

CPLPs have been successfully implemented in both public and private schools at the elementary and secondary levels, and the overall response to the projects has been positive. Some participants even recommended that the CPLP be expanded to cover other subjects. Parents and children stated that beyond learning music content, they were pleased to note the added benefit of simply spending time together and dialoguing.

It is important to note that there is no one answer to the question of how to get parents involved in their children's learning. No one maintains that it is easy to get parents involved, but it is certainly worth the try. Implementing a CPLP in your school could be an effective way to involve parents in a substantive way. Why not plan on implementing a CPLP that puts the emphasis on positive reinforcement in learning rather than tying learning to grades?

CPLP and Your Administrator

Meet with your administrator and be prepared with a tentative outline that anticipates questions by answering the following:

- What are the purposes of the project?
- What concepts and skills will the parents and students be learning?

- How is project content connected with instruction and local, state, and national standards of learning?
- How will parents and students be assessed?
- How long will the project last?
- How will the project affect students' grades?
- What about parents and students who do not choose to participate?
- How are you going to communicate with parents and students?
- What will your parent letter of invitation contain? (Have a sample letter ready.)

Assure the administrator that you will submit for his or her approval any written communication with parents. Be prepared to name the benefits of parent involvement. In addition to these benefits, your administrator may be pleased to be involved in the project because it helps to prepare students for standards of learning testing by being integrated with other subject areas. In addition, the project provides a clear example of effective school-home collaboration that helps to enrich school reaccreditation reports.

CPLP in Your School

After getting the blessing of your administrator, work to keep the project short, simple, and focused. Then meet with parents, distribute the invitation letter, and answer any questions they might have.

Start the project making sure that you involve parents and students working together right away with an easy assignment that is to be turned in within the first week. One teacher used a quick five-question quiz with questions that were not particularly connected to the project, but simply got the parent and student conversing. Parent and student asked each other: "What kind of music do you like to listen to the most?" "Who is your favorite artist?" "If you could play any instrument, what would it be?" "What kind of music calms you down?" "What kind of music do you wish you knew more about?"

As the project progresses, send an encouraging letter home at the halfway mark (or, in an ideal world, meet with parents and students together) and remind participants that they are doing well, citing actual instances of creativity. The week before the end of the project, send another encouraging letter home reporting on progress made and reminding parents and students of the culminating activity and awards time. Keep your administrator informed all along the way and invite her to this activity. You may even want to give her a study packet and quizzes to complete alone or with a student, or even with you! As the project nears completion, prepare certificates of achievement for parents and students signed by you and the administrator, and coordinate an event with refreshments where students and parents receive the certificates from the administrator.

Parent-Student Quizzes

Remember that the purposes of the quizzes are really to provide reinforcement for concepts and skills; to build connections between parent, child, and school; and to increase content knowledge and improve listening and performance skills. You won't be able to do all of that with every quiz, but keep focused on the purposes of the CPLP.

Keep the quizzes short and focused on important content items. To enliven the process, include a few fun facts in the study materials. Extra credit could be given for those items on the quizzes. For a self-assessment approach, supply answers upside down at the bottom of the page or on the back of the quiz with instructions: "Play fair! Wait until you are finished, and then look only to check your answers." Prepare quizzes for students to give parents and vice versa. Or use the same quiz, which they take separately, and then exchange papers to grade. Consider giving a pretest and a posttest to provide some evidence of individual achievement level change after involvement in the CPLP.

Parent, Student, and Teacher Surveys

Allow plenty of time for parents to complete the surveys. You will have to contact some of them with a reminder. Really try hard to get as many surveys as possible returned so you can more accurately assess the attitudes of the parents relative to the effectiveness of the CPLP. The surveys used for the following sample CPLPs included statements that covered the purposes of the CPLP: strengthening parent-student-school relations, increasing content knowledge, and improving listening and performance skills. The survey also asked parents to offer suggestions for ways to improve the project. It is most effective to have students complete the student survey in class. Students at all levels are more likely to stay on task if the teacher reads the questions to them. For older students, parents, and the teacher, use a Likert-type rating scale containing five degrees of agreement with each statement: 1 = strongly disagree, 2 = somewhat disagree, 3 = neither agree nor disagree, 4 = somewhat agree, and 5 = strongly agree. For younger students, simplify the statements. For these students, in place of the Likert-type scale use a happy face, a neutral face, and a sad face. Do not expect kindergarten students to be able to fill out the survey, but you might find it productive to talk about the project with them to find out their attitudes toward it.

Create Your Own CPLP

The following template may be useful in creating your own CPLP.

1. Choose a target group: chorus, band, orchestra, general music.
2. Choose a grade level.

3. Decide on a CPLP title.

4. List content you want your students to teach their parents.

5. List items for a home study packet; examples are flash cards, directed listening activity or checklist, performance task, quiz, answer key, information sheet with contact information, timeline for project, links to listening sites.

6. List ways for the student to quiz the parent and for the parent to quiz the student. For example, provide the same quiz for both parent and child to take separately and then discuss; separate quizzes for comparison; or flash-card quiz for parent and child to take and then compare and discuss results.

7. Determine project length. Two to five weeks is best. Student interest lags beyond that.

8. Name culminating activity, if any. For example, coordinate with other subject teachers and engage a visiting artist or group, or invite a knowledgeable parent (e.g., native of the country you are studying) to make a presentation. Other ideas include a field trip to a performance that links with project content, or a group presentation or performance that includes the participating parents.

The following example demonstrates how a CPLP fits this template. This project was effectively implemented in three third-grade public school music classes.

Sample Project

Music and the Ancient Mali: African Music and Culture

Overview (Classroom Music, Grade 3)

This project took place over the course of five weeks, one music class meeting per week. The project was chosen because all third-grade students would be studying ancient Mali as part of their regular classroom instruction. They would be tested on this content knowledge during standards testing in the spring. In addition, third graders would perform at the school's annual Multicultural Night, and a portion of the project would be used in the performance.

The students were introduced to the music of Mali by listening to compact discs, viewing websites, reading online encyclopedia articles, and reviewing content from third-grade classroom state standards packets as compiled by the school district.

After the students studied the content from the standards packet, they were given a music class packet to take home. This packet was intended for students to use in studying with their parents the content they learned in the music classroom. The home study packet included the following:

- flashcards for parents and students to use in testing each other on the following terms and names: Mali, Sundiata, traditional African music, djembe, balafon, kora, griot, Diabate', Kamissoko, and Kouyate';
- a world map showing where Mali is located;
- pictures of instruments traditionally used to make Mali music along with a CD featuring these instruments; and
- a quiz for parents and students to take separately and then exchange and discuss.

The last question on the quiz asked parents to act as a *griot* (storyteller) for their family. Griots have been an important part of West African society since ancient times. They act as historians and genealogists to noble families throughout West Africa, including Mali. These griots often use music to tell their stories. For this last quiz question, the parent-griots were asked to write down important family traditions. Rhythms were composed from phrases taken from these traditions. The rhythms were then used as ostinati played on mallet instruments to accompany the chorus performance on Multicultural Night. The final activity was a field trip to a local theater to experience a performance by a storyteller who sang and played the kora and djembe.

Survey Highlights

The feedback from the surveys showed that almost all parents somewhat agreed or strongly agreed that the CPLP strengthened their relationships with the school and student. Almost all students agreed that the CPLP strengthened their school-parent-teacher relationship. Almost all parents somewhat agreed or strongly agreed that the CPLP provided new knowledge and helped them understand what their students were learning in music. In all of the statements, almost all of the students agreed that the CPLP provided positive, fruitful experiences. The teacher somewhat agreed or strongly agreed with all of the survey statements, although she was neutral or somewhat agreed in the parent-student-school relationship category. In assessing the project itself, all participants somewhat agreed or strongly agreed that the CPLP should be continued with another project and strongly agreed that other schools could benefit from a CPLP.

Notable Quotes from Teacher, Parent, and Student Surveys

Teacher Comments from the Surveys

- "I'd like to try an evening program where students and their parents learn, and then sing or play music together."
- "I enjoyed creating a new unit of study to coordinate with classroom instruction."
- "I welcomed the increased contact with parents."
- "I would like to try a performance practice CPLP in the future."

Parent Comments from the Surveys

Changes

- "Add dances by using a DVD rather than music CD only."
- "Include more music from other parts of the world."
- "Use shorter versions of music."
- "Supply video plus audio so I could see the instruments being played."

Benefits

- "Having my child teach me, giving us time together in his learning."
- "Doing this with my energetic, excited, eager child. He couldn't wait to get started quizzing me on the flashcards. This was fun!"
- "The time spent with my son. He was a very good teacher, very task-minded. Loved the music, the pictures, and the map."
- "I enjoyed having my daughter teach me something I knew nothing about."
- "It was great to see a connection between social studies and music."
- "I really liked how the music curriculum is related to their classroom curriculum to give a richer, broader knowledge base."
- "This initiative is an excellent way to involve parents in a fun and entertaining way, in the interests and education of their children."
- "It was fun working with my daughter and switching places. She really enjoyed grading my paper and telling me to be a better listener. (I had to ask her to repeat several things.)"
- "I really enjoyed being instructed by my child. Teaching something is the best way to reinforce and ascertain understanding. I would like to see the project broadened to cover more subjects."

Student Comments from the Surveys

- "I benefited most from spending time with my parents."
- "Maybe put more in so it could take a tad longer and be more fun. . . . CPLP rules!"
- "I would like that it would take a little less time (not that it took too long)."
- "Thank you, Mrs. R., for teaching us this stuff."
- "Learning that music is saying something. It is not just nice music."
- "I like music class a lot. I wish to have more. Signed: The Coolest Student."

Tips for CPLP Success

- Involve your administrator early and often. Cite benefits such as accreditation and registration, public relations, research-based evidence that increased parent involvement has a positive effect on attendance, discipline, grade advancement, higher scores in subjects such as reading and math.
- Inform parents early and often. Informed parents are happier parents. A face-to-face meeting is best combined with an information letter. Supply specific expectations; for example, specify how much of the parents' time the project will take, starting and ending dates, the purposes of the project, and how the project will affect student grades.
- The first project is important. Construct it so parents will want to be involved again. They do talk with each other!
- Keep it simple, short, and focused. Don't try to teach too much in one project.
- Base the CPLP on content you are already going to cover. Why reinvent the wheel?
- Connect your project with learning in another subject area and standards of learning from the arts and other disciplines (National Standards for Music Education, State Standards of Learning).
- Focus on fun learning and provide positive rewards; for example, present a certificate of achievement to parents and students on completion of the project.
- Use a website to provide information, listening examples, links to resources, and reinforcement of concepts and skills.
- Use a culminating activity with refreshments to provide reinforcement, camaraderie, and a sense of accomplishment for all participants.

Additional Sample Connecting Parents with Learning Projects

Sample CPLP 1

Join the Rhythm Kingdom (Elementary or Middle School Band, Chorus, Orchestra, or General Music Class)

The Rhythm Kingdom project is most suitable for elementary and middle school students. For a high school CPLP, try band, chorus, or orchestra Olympics with gold, silver, or bronze categories for achievement. Use Olympic "events" that focus on rhythms taken from the performance literature or quizzes on the historical background of pieces performed. Parents and students can quiz each other in these areas and earn medals or certificates. You may be surprised at how this type of reinforcement using tangible rewards can be successful at all grade levels.

Rhythm Kingdom

Students and parents work to achieve passing scores on rhythm tests for promotion through four levels.

Project time: Four ten-week quarters. Can also work effectively for just one quarter.

All students and parents begin as Knights or Ladies and then can earn promotion to the following:

- Baron/Baroness
- Earl/Countess
- Duke/Duchess
- King/Queen

1. Students learn meter signature and the rhythm of the week taken from music studied in class or rehearsal.
2. Students teach parents the meter signature and then the rhythm of the week by demonstrating how to clap and count a steady beat, then how to clap and count the rhythm. Student and parent practice alone and then together.

3. Student and parent take the examination (two chances for parent, two chances for student).
   - Parent claps steady beat and student performs rhythm of the week and is graded by parent using the following Rhythm Scoring Guide.
   - Student claps steady beat and parent performs the rhythm of the week and is graded by student using the following Rhythm Scoring Guide.

Rhythm Scoring Guide

1 = all rhythms accurate and aligned with the beat
2 = almost all rhythms accurate and aligned with the beat
*********************** Promotion Cut***************************
3 = some rhythms accurate and somewhat near the beat
4 = few rhythms accurate and not near the beat
5 = no rhythms accurate and nowhere near the beat
   - Promotion periods consist of four ten-week periods.
   - Students turn in scores each week.
   - At the conclusion of each ten-week period, titles are awarded with certificates.
   - Total average score of 1 or 2 earns a promotion of one title.
   - Everyone gets a certificate with a title but not everyone earns a promotion.
   - Certificates are signed by teacher and principal.

At the conclusion of the project, parents and students complete a survey to assess the effectiveness of the CPLP's three areas of emphasis:

1. Strengthen parent-student-school relations.
2. Increase content knowledge.
3. Improve listening and performance skills.

❧

Sample CPLP 2

Rhythm Reading and Composition (Elementary School Classroom Music— Six-Week Project)

Students invite their parents to participate in a voluntary six-week project in which they will learn rhythm skills as well as create a simple musical composition. This project complements the beginning study of rhythm reading as applied to learning recorders while reinforcing elements of music study in the music classroom.

Project Outline

Week 1: Getting Started

Parent and student interview each other about their musical interests. The purpose of the interviews is to open up a dialogue about musical matters between the parent and student. These interviews also provide an easy, non-threatening assignment that gets the parent and student involved together in the project right away.

Week 2: Sound Discovery and Musical Conversation

Parent and student use recorders supplied by the school. This project assumes that students have received recorder instruction previously so they are able to teach parents how to produce a characteristic tone, and how to finger and place on a staff the notes B, A, and G. For five to ten minutes, parent and student use any of these three pitches to take turns playing and echoing short rhythms lasting four to six seconds each. Students give short, oral progress reports to the teacher indicating any problems encountered and noting successes.

Week 3: Introducing Basic Rhythm Notation

Teacher constructs and provides parent and student with Note Values worksheets to complete. These sheets contain whole note through eighth note values. The student instructs the parent on how to draw and count each of the notes. Afterward, they work separately writing down different rhythm combinations of note values to complete two measures, four beats each. They discuss their answers and discover who was able to write down the most rhythm combinations to complete the measures. The student and parent grade each other's worksheet relative to rhythm and beat accuracy for each measure. The student returns the completed sheets to the teacher who reviews them for accuracy. On the board, students notate rhythms from the completed worksheets, and the class counts and claps them, accompanied by selected students who provide a steady pulse on rhythm instruments.

Week 4: Performing Basic Rhythm Notation

Using the Note Values worksheet from Week 3, the student teaches the parent how to perform the rhythms to a steady pulse. Parent pats a steady pulse while the student claps the rhythms, and then they reverse the process. They discuss and assess performance accuracy. They repeat the process playing the rhythms on their recorders, selecting either B, A, or G. Students give short, oral reports to the teacher noting any problems and successes.

Week 5: Sound and Silence

Parent and student learn rests (whole through eighth) using a teacher-prepared worksheet containing note and rest values. Parent and student then each write four four-beat measures of music using B, A, G, and a variety of rhythms starting and ending on G. They place note names over each note and perform their compositions on their recorders. Parent and student grade each other's composition relative to the accurate number beats in each measure. Compositions are then turned in to the teacher for a final review.

Week 6: Survey Completion and Project Culmination

At the conclusion of the project, parents and students complete a survey to assess the effectiveness of the CPLP's three areas of emphasis:

1. Strengthen parent-student-school relations.
2. Increase content knowledge.
3. Improve listening and performance skills.

Certificate of Completion awards are distributed by the teacher and principal at a gathering of participating parents and students.

~

The CPLP and a Diverse Student Body

The United States has always been a country of immigrants. With the influx of families from a wide range of countries comes the challenge of communicating with students and parents whose first language might not be English. In an attempt to help students, school systems have put programs in place that contain sequential curriculum strands that teach English as a second language. Other approaches have also been made to improve communication between the school and home. For example, it is now common to have written communication from school districts appear in several languages. This procedure is better than what one of my university students encountered when he arrived from overseas not all that long ago. He spent a great deal of time trying to get documents from the local school district translated so his parents could sign them knowledgeably. But even with a growing awareness on the part of schools and teacher training programs of the increasing diversity of the United States, there still exist high barriers to learning when families arrive from other countries. In addition to the language, there are unfamiliar customs and a mix of cultures that can dramatically hinder learning.

The CPLP is an effective way to connect with families of other cultures because the students instruct the parents and a natural pathway to the school is opened. In all of our teaching we realize that there is no magic wand and no single way to involve parents; however, parents who are learning content along with their children will surely benefit our programs substantially. Meaningful and enduring results can take place if we get even a few parents to connect with learning.[9]

Communication Essential to Effectiveness

In the vitally important area of communication, artistry and attitude meet. Command of content and mastery of methods combine with your attributes of attitude to make it possible for students to learn. Your teaching will become more effective if you know your subject intimately, use a variety of teaching strategies to help students understand, and connect with your students as individuals. Caring, trust, and respect, combined with all the other positive attributes of attitude you possess, will keep the conduits of communication open between you, your students, parents, and the community. Through these conduits will come increased opportunities for growth for all students.

Communication and Your Job Interview

In anticipation of their first interview for a music teaching position, aspiring teachers always seem to be concerned about what the interviewers are looking for. In the book *Communication: Making Connections*, Seiler and Beall cite communication skills (verbal and written) as the most important quality that employers seek.[10] Your interviewers will surely focus on how you relate to others.

During the course of the questioning, interviewers will be imagining you in a number of situations that are part and parcel of teaching. The interviewers will be thinking of how you will interact with very bright students who might dominate a class, how you will react to reluctant, truculent students, abrasive parents, other teachers, building administration, the community at large, special learners, and students from other countries. They will be thinking about how you will handle administrative tasks such as documenting parent contacts, and maintaining attendance registers and other student records. In each instance your attitude involving communication skills, will be of utmost importance. Recall the ABCs of attitude and reflect on how you will use these to communicate effectively with each of these encounters and tasks.

Interviewers will keep the following questions in their minds as they speak with you, audition you, review your teaching portfolio, and observe you teach a demonstration lesson: Is the candidate a competent musician? Does the candidate know the subject content thoroughly? Does the candidate know how to use this content in designing lessons? Does the candidate have at the ready a variety of methods and strategies for implementing each lesson? Does the candidate demonstrate the ability or the potential to communicate content to a wide variety of student types? Does the candidate's nonverbal communication support or contradict what the candidate is saying? Does the candidate exhibit the potential for verbal and nonverbal communication skills that will be necessary to use with the network that surrounds each student—family, administration, other teachers, and community? Does the candidate speak well and present a professional appearance? What positive attributes of attitude does this candidate exhibit that will help establish positive, productive relationships with all students and all parts of the school community? What sort of character traits does the candidate exhibit that we want our students to emulate?

Out of all of these questions, if the ones concerning communication skills cannot be satisfactorily answered, then the candidate's viability as a contender for the position will be in jeopardy *even if the other questions are satisfactorily answered.* Your success as an effective music teacher depends on effective communication, and effective communication depends on the effective combination of artistry and attitude.

Summary

Communication is where the combination of artistry and attitude plays out in real-life situations. Pledge to yourself that you will work to become an adept communicator. An adept communicator is one who dialogues freely and exhibits cooperation and understanding with all constituent groups, cultivates a natural sense of humor, and knows how to lead students to learn how to learn by involving them in gaining ownership of what they are studying. An adept communicator regularly asks students to engage in personal and group creativity, analyzes what they are doing, and offers suggestions for change. An adept communicator effectively uses nonverbal communication to provide clarity, support, and reinforcement of the verbal messages of instruction, and addresses individual student needs through consistent assessments. An adept communicator uses the results of these assessments to develop a variety of teaching strategies that fit each student's personality and knows how to create a positive learning atmosphere by establishing a nurturing rapport with all students.

$\backsim$

Six Components of Effective Teaching

As important as communication is in effective teaching, it serves as but one component among others. For our purposes, I have included five other areas derived from the research literature and experience that, along with the component of communication, should act as essential elements of what makes your teaching effective.

The following list contains six components of effective teaching along with how each one functions in the teaching and learning context. These six components will be referenced and used in following chapters.

1. Content
   - Mastering subject and technical skills
   - Knowing high-quality literature and materials
2. Communication
   - Exhibiting cooperation and understanding
   - Displaying a natural sense of humor
   - Knowing ways to create a positive learning atmosphere
   - Knowing how to lead students to learn how to learn
   - Involving all students in gaining ownership of what they are studying
   - Addressing student needs by knowing a variety of teaching strategies
   - Connecting with all components of the students' constituent network
3. Comprehension
   - Setting high standards and giving students the tools to meet or surpass them
   - Knowing how to measure student achievement accurately and usefully
   - Using student outcomes to measure your teaching effectiveness
4. Dedication
   - To the success of all types of students
   - To excellence and academic rigor
   - To your own professional growth

5. Structure
   - Consistency
   - Planning and preparation
   - Organization and management (people and paper)
6. Character
   - Trust and respect
   - Reasonableness and fairness
   - Ethics and values
   - Honor and integrity
   - Walking your talk

As shown in chapter 1, research studies on effective music teaching over the decades have identified scores of traits that are quite similar. These traits from the research along with the traits of effective teachers you have had demonstrate a striking blend of artistry and attitude. Command of content and mastery of methods are apparent together with a range of attitudinal traits.

Typical recurring traits derived from the research literature and from experience appear in the following list. To see how these teacher traits and the six components align, match each of the bulleted traits in the following list to each of the six components of effective teaching listed previously. Individually or as a class, list or name as many of the following traits that complement each component. Each component should be supported by at least one of the following traits.

- Enthusiasm
- Care
- Master-level communication
- Hard work
- Energy
- Compassion
- Consistency
- Organization
- Passion
- Clear expectations
- A positive attitude
- A personal interest in individual student success
- A sense of humor
- Management
- Perseverance
- High standards

- Professional growth: reflection, reevaluation, revision of all aspects of instructional delivery

As a result of this exercise, it should be apparent that traits of effective teachers support and are closely aligned with the six components. Keep these six components in mind because you will meet them again as you examine effective teaching and leadership, and as you construct your personal philosophy of music education in later chapters.

In the next chapter you will discover the importance of well-developed communication skills in the area of leadership by examining types of leaders and by reviewing case studies of leaders who are proven effective. You will also see how effective leaders function in the context of the six components of effective teaching.

For Reflection, Discussion, Assignment

1. Review one article from the resources at the end of this chapter, outline its main points using bullets, and explain how you will use the information in your teaching.
2. Choose, or be assigned, one group from the following, and name and explain two ways you would improve communication with the members of that group: (1) administrators, (2) fellow teachers and building staff, (3) parents, and (4) music and nonmusic students.
3. Using the ABCs of attitude from chapter 4, identify and discuss five attributes that you might use to improve communication. How would you use these five attributes? Provide real or hypothetical examples.
4. To improve your nonverbal communication skills, have someone make a video of you as you present a five- to seven-minute classroom oral report using any of the articles from the Resources section, or any article on communication and learning that is approved by your instructor. You might be surprised to recognize some of the behaviors mentioned in this chapter. Invite your classmates to offer a critique of the message and the meaning. Focus on eye and facial expression, body language, vocal tone and volume, and verbal and physical "tics." Did the presentation reinforce the meaning or send confusing or contradictory messages?
5. Present a brief report on nonverbal communication you have observed from watching people interacting in any public venue—restaurant, coffee shop, sporting event (players and spectators), concert performers and audience, or library. Report on messages and meanings, conflict and congruence conveyed by the nonverbal behaviors displayed.

6. Interview a teacher from any level—kindergarten through university—and ask him or her to identify five effective communication techniques he or she uses to connect effectively with students, parents (if applicable), administrators, fellow teachers, staff, other students, and community.

7. Interview a university student from any subject area and have the student complete the sentence: "The teachers who communicated with me most effectively and helped me to learn used the following approach(es). . . ."

8. Using the template from the "Connecting Parents with Learning Project" section in this chapter, create one project for the high school level (grades 9–12). Choose band, chorus, or orchestra, or consider creating a project for other high school courses such as special ensembles (e.g., jazz groups, mariachi band, steel band), or classes such as theory, electronic music, guitar, or general music. Be prepared to explain how you would implement the CPLP, including possible problems you might encounter.

9. Using the template from the "Connecting Parents with Learning Project" section, create one project for the middle school level (grades 5–8) classroom music or performing ensemble. Be prepared to explain how you would implement the CPLP, including possible problems you might encounter. For the middle school classroom consider general music, guitar, piano class, or other classes such as electronic music. For performing ensembles consider band, chorus, or orchestra, or create a project for other ensembles such as jazz band, marching band, jazz choir, show choir, or musical production.

10. Using the template from the "Connecting Parents with Learning Project" section, create one project for the K–4 elementary level classroom music or performing ensemble. Be prepared to explain how you would implement it, including possible problems you might encounter.

Resources

Anderson, Brian. "Sending the Right Message." *Teaching Music* 3, no. 3 (December 1995): 38–39.

Arnold, William E., and Lynne McClure. *Communication Training and Development*, 2nd ed. Prospect Heights, IL: Waveland Press, 1996.

Battersby, Sharyn L. "Increasing Awareness in the General Music Classroom." *General Music Today* 22, no. 3 (Spring 2009): 14–18.

Bobestsky, Victor. "Turn Parents into Partners." *Teaching Music* 11, no. 1 (2003): 38–41.

Burton, Suzanne L. "Educate Our Advocates." *Music Educators Journal* 90, no. 5 (2004): 17–21.

Cane, Susannah. "Collaboration with Music: A Noteworthy Endeavor." *Music Educators Journal* 96, no. 1 (September 2009): 33–39.

Catt, Stephen, Donald Miller, and Ken Schallenkamp. "You Are the Key: Communicate for Learning Effectiveness." *Education* 127, no. 3 (Spring 2007): 369–77.

Conderman, Greg, Sarah Johnston-Rodriquez, Paula Hartman, and Drew Kemp. "What Teachers Should Say and How They Should Say It." *Kappa Delta Pi Record* 46, no. 4 (Summer 2010): 175–81.

Epstein, Joyce L. *School, Family and Community Partnerships: Preparing Educators and Improving Schools.* Boulder, CO: Westview Press, 2001.

Guilbert, Juiliette. "Teach Your Parents Well." *Teacher Magazine* 18, no. 3 (November/December 2006): 32–37.

Hiatt-Michael, Diane. *Preparing Teachers to Work with Parents.* Washington, DC: ERIC Clearinghouse on Teaching and Teacher Education, 2001, www.ericdigests.org/2002-3/parents.html.

——. *Promising Practices for Family Involvement in School.* Greenwich, CT: Information Age, 2001.

——. *Promising Practices for Teachers to Engage Families of English Language Learners.* Greenwich, CT: Information Age, 2007.

Mostovoy, Stephanie. "Students Learn by Teaching Their Parents." *Teaching Music* 8 (February 2001): 32–36.

Nowmos, Christine M. "Using Informance to Educate Parents and Demonstrate the Learning Process." *General Music Today* 23, no. 3 (April 2010): 5–14.

Polinak, Susan. "Working with Proactive Parents." *Teaching Music* 18, no. 2 (October 2010): 38–43.

Seiller, William J., and Melissa L. Beall. *Communication: Making Connections,* 7th ed. New York: Pearson Education, 2008.

Sindberg, Laura K. "Intentions and Perceptions: In Search of Alignment." *Music Educators Journal* 95, no. 4 (June 2009): 18–22.

Smar, Benedict J. "6 Ways to Partner with Parents and Community." *Teaching Music* 10, no. 2 (October 2002): 48–53.

Townsend, Alfred S. "Building Shared Goals in the High School Music Department." *Teaching Music* 14, no. 3 (December 2006): 48–51.

——. "Common Missteps of New Teachers." *The Instrumentalist* 64, no. 2 (September 2009): 28–30, 56.

——. "Implement a 'Connecting Parents with Learning Project' in Your School." *Music Educators Journal* 97, no. 1 (September 2010): 45–48.

U.S. Department of Education. "Engaging Parents in Education: Lessons from Five Parental Information and Resource Centers." 2007, www.ed.gov/admins/comm/parents/parentinvolve/engagingparents.pdf.

6

Effective Leadership

Leading well is not about enriching yourself—it's about empowering others.[1]

Effective leadership is effective teaching. From the boardroom to the classroom to the rehearsal room the qualities of effective leaders are the same as those of the effective teacher. There is no *effective* leadership apart from effective teaching and there is no *effective* teaching apart from effective leadership. How can one lead without being an effective teacher and how can one teach without being an effective leader?

The very essence of teaching is leading. Leading is causing students to learn, and empowering them to learn how to learn; enabling them to discover truth and gain knowledge; piquing their intellectual and creative curiosity; inspiring them to succeed; uncovering potential they didn't know they had; building character and confidence; guiding them to become active, productive global artist-citizens; setting high goals and maintaining academic rigor while providing all students with the tools to achieve those goals; having a vision of success for each student; and persevering in the face of all obstacles. The list could go on and on. Recall the effective music teacher traits from the first chapter, and you will notice that these traits are accurate, useful descriptors of leaders and teachers alike. However, knowing how these traits work together to lead students is the key. It is developing a leadership style that encompasses a range of applications to suit different situations and the needs of individual students. It is maintaining the ability to assess the results of your leadership and use the results to effect change in your teaching and in student learning, and it is developing leadership in your students so they gain ownership of the teaching and learning process.

Types of Leaders

There are many different types of leaders who exhibit a range of styles. Out of these, for our purposes, I have chosen two extremes that can hinder learning and will provide a sharp contrast to the third type of leader we will examine. The two extremes of leadership are the dictator leader and the country club leader. The third type of leader is the servant leader. Under the dictator leader and the country club leader, some things do get done and some progress can occur. But at what cost? Think about how much more could have been accomplished if the leadership styles of these two types had been connected to the development of the whole student instead of being focused elsewhere.

The Dictator Leader

If you have ever served under a dictator leader, you have experienced a top-down style where the leader issues orders and the subordinates are expected to carry them out. There is seldom any opportunity for anything other than one-way communication. Suggestions are not encouraged, and assessment of outcomes is done unilaterally by the leader. Some would say that this type of leader is a military type of leader, but in the military the most successful leaders are those who not only issue orders but also listen well, are concerned about morale and individual achievement, and are quick to spread the praise around for a job well done. They do issue orders, but they are vitally engaged with both the heads and hearts of their troops. Dictator leaders are different. They are often micromanagers who feel that only they can do any job right, no matter how small, so they hover and hound and raise counterproductive anxiety levels. Their students never truly take ownership of performances or classroom activities because this type of leader can't let go of controlling even the tiniest bit of any activity. Dictator leaders are full of hurtful pride because if the students do well, they take all of the credit. If the students do poorly, they often are quick to shift the blame to issues they claim are beyond their control. The needs of the students and their growth do not get top priority. Ego does.

The Country Club Leader

You can usually tell a country club leader because this type of leader cultivates a serene demeanor at all costs. Country club leaders are passive and are interested primarily in keeping the peace, maintaining the status quo, and going along to get along. These leaders are not so much concerned with setting and achieving high goals for the students as in not letting the job get in the way of other interests. The students are generally happy because there aren't many demands placed on them, and their students produce predictable, mediocre work. Country club leaders can be quite sociable, and they do communicate frequently with the students and their support network; however, this is done to ensure that there are no ruffled feathers to be smoothed. Students pass through country club leaders' classrooms or ensembles without finding much inspiration.

The Servant Leader

Then there is the servant leader. The term *servant leader* embodies the aspects of those leaders who place the organization and the needs of others ahead of their own. The servant leader is one whose style is marked by active collaboration and effective communication. This leader's style is one of conciliation and a commitment to the growth of the whole student. The servant leader can only be truly effective by combining these admirable traits with the commitment to be persistent in setting and achieving significant goals. All of these characteristics of the servant leader align seamlessly with the traits of effective teaching discussed in previous chapters.

I once saw a sign on a coach's desk that read, "There is no limit to how far we can go if it doesn't matter who gets the credit." That is precisely the attitude servant leaders have and project to all those around them. Rather than focusing on themselves and their accomplishments, they focus on causing students to realize and use to the fullest extent their abilities and other special qualities. Servant leaders have a clear vision supported by a strong, purposeful commitment to fulfilling that vision. They are knowledgeable about their subject, communicate well, maintain academic rigor, and lead by example—by how they act, by what they say, and by what they do. Servant leaders are unafraid to embrace honest self-appraisal that leads to growth. Finally, these leaders give up their ego for the sake of raising their students' progress and achievement. The servant leader models and develops the component of character in all of the above. "The bottom line in leadership isn't how far we advance ourselves but how far we advance others."[2]

Student Leaders

Teachers who are effective servant leaders want their students to assume leadership roles. There are the "official" roles of classroom project leaders and officers of groups. Other leadership positions include ensemble section leaders, student conductors, equipment coordinators, and drum majors. De facto leaders include principal roles in the musical production or class play and soloists with ensembles. But what about the students who are not involved in these more prominent leadership positions? We want them also to develop qualities of leadership. I am sure that you want your students to put aside a "me first and only" attitude, and strive for excellence and the success of the group through hard work and persistence. All of your students will grow as leaders and world citizens by developing these and other sterling character traits such as honesty, trustworthiness, caring, and self-control. If you develop all of your students as leaders, the more formal leadership positions will be filled by students who already know what the essential traits of a leader are. How will you develop such leaders?

Student leaders reflect the way they have been led. Student leaders who serve under a dictator type will try to lead by just ordering others around. Those types of leaders can accomplish some things, but their influence is limited because they have to stay right on top of every detail in order to make sure things get done their way. True teamwork and ownership is absent with this type of student leader, and any progress toward meeting goals is typically short lived.

Student leaders who have been a product of the country club leader focus on the social aspects of their position at the expense of vision, goal setting, and achievement. This type of student leader can get others to join in for entertaining activities, but without a clearly stated mission and commitment to success, students drop in and out, and only keep a loose, largely unproductive connection with the organization. Groups with this type of student leader will likely wander and flounder.

The servant leader who places the good of the order ahead of personal gain is in the best position to develop true, effective student leaders who themselves exhibit the characteristics of effective teachers. Servant leaders, however, are not "shrinking violets." They set specific goals, issue directives, and hold students accountable, but these things are always aligned with student needs, and balanced with a genuine interest and involvement in the success of each student. Building positive relationships with each student will provide a productive base for leadership development.

The most powerful way to develop student leadership is to model consistently the characteristics of a true leader that we have reviewed. It is remarkable to notice how observant students are and how strongly they imitate the behavior of their teachers. I have seen students completely change the way they act within the few minutes it takes to go from one teacher to another. The same students who with one teacher act responsibly and respectfully can change behavior in the blink of an eye. How can that happen? It is all about the culture of character and leadership that the teacher persists in modeling and expecting from the students. Effective teachers never, ever give up working to create this culture in the classroom or rehearsal hall. They are successful because they not only serve as consistent examples of the desired behaviors but also show their appreciation when their students demonstrate those behaviors. This positive reinforcement will go a long way in establishing a classroom atmosphere free of distraction and conducive to learning.

Student leaders can also be developed if you design and implement lessons that enable students to gain ownership of the process and product. In the classroom, this can be accomplished by group activities that engage students in taking the concepts and skills they have learned and applying them to new projects that they now own. In ensembles, students can gain ownership by being asked to provide suggestions for improvement of their performance. This can be done during full or sectional rehearsals, and in postconcert review sessions.

If you have made the effort to create fertile soil for leadership in your classroom by treating all of your students as potential leaders, students will sprout and bloom naturally. In addition to the personality traits, and the other qualities covered in this chapter, it would be wise to make sure your prospective student leaders can understand and answer the question "Do you just want to be a leader, or do you want to do the things a leader does?" In other words, "Do you want all of a sudden to be called a master carpenter without doing anything that a master carpenter does to earn that title, or, in addition to creating beautiful woodwork, are you willing to carry lumber, get splinters, clean up the job site, and bang your thumb with a hammer?" Your students should be able to give a positive answer to this question before starting their leadership journey.

As you develop student leaders, don't necessarily focus on their performance ability, but rather concentrate on what they might offer as leaders based on their communication skills, independent problem solving, and goal-setting and attainment ability, along with evidence of understanding what responsibility means.

Leadership and Six Components of Effective Teaching

True leadership and effective teaching are indissolubly connected. Remember the six components of effective teaching to which you were introduced in the previous chapter. As was explained, these six components are derived from effective teaching research. Each of these components is now presented as it connects to your development as a servant leader.

Content

Effective leaders know their subject matter inside and out. They are convinced that they must know in depth what they are teaching in order to lead their students on a productive pathway. With limited content knowledge they can lead their students only so far. If they are uncertain about what they are teaching, their students will also become uncertain. This can lead to a negative learning atmosphere, and lack of trust and confidence.

Effective leaders continually seek professional growth in knowledge of high-quality literature, and they spend time studying scores and practicing conducting. They keep up to date in classroom best practices and are always looking for quality song literature that has artistic integrity, diversity, and authenticity. By regularly interacting with colleagues, reading journals, and attending conference workshops, they gain new ways for their students to understand concepts and skills. They seek to develop their facility in a range of methodologies such as those developed by Orff, Kodaly, Dalcroze, Suzuki, and Gordon. They connect history and world cultures to what they teach. They are adept at and never stop pursuing a deeper knowledge of vocal and instrumental techniques and rehearsal strategies. In all, through solid content knowledge effective leaders build a strong foundation for connecting their students to learning.

Communication

Effective leaders develop multiple variations of their teaching styles to fit the many personalities of their students. Their leadership is propelled by understanding what the individual characteristics of each student are that will affect learning. They are sensitive to the outside influences that make up their students' worlds, and they include them in fashioning effective strategies for learning.

Recall from earlier chapters that communication involves a host of skills that connect teacher, student, and the students' support network, all driven by attributes of attitude. Effective leaders are adept at establishing and maintaining open dialogue with all of the constituent groups that surround and feed into the day-to-day school experience. Use the ABCs of attitude from chapter 4 to propel your communication. It is impossible for a leader to lead without a finely tuned sense of communication. Leadership and communication work together with comprehension in that student understanding reveals the effectiveness of your communication.

Comprehension

Effective leadership includes regular self-assessment and student assessment. To test your effectiveness as a leader, evaluate the results of your teaching. Ask yourself, "How are my lessons and teaching strategies working to improve student learning?" Use national and state standards of learning as benchmarks of achievement, but do not rely solely on those. Student success depends on so much more than just meeting standards of learning. By recognizing and rewarding progress rather than just the end result, your assessments will provide necessary feedback for you and your students so that authentic growth can occur—learning how to learn. Your effectiveness as a leader will grow as you regularly assess your students and use the results for curriculum modification and adjustment in your teaching approaches.

Dedication

You will inspire your students by exhibiting a wholehearted commitment to their success within the school walls, and by exhibiting your concern for their well being even when not in your music class or ensemble rehearsal. One band director I know is very demanding of her students, yet every student knows that this director will never ask them to do something that she is unwilling to do herself. They know that even though she sets high goals, she will always provide them with ways to achieve those goals, and that she sincerely and deeply appreciates the efforts her students make to meet her demands. Finally, and perhaps more importantly, every single one of her students knows that she will be there for them at all times. If on Christmas Eve one of her students had been injured in a car accident, everyone knows that this teacher would be there at the hospital providing comfort and whatever was needed to take care of her student and the family.

Dedicated, effective leaders also inspire their students by continuing to make music themselves by practicing and performing regularly. In everything they do, effective leaders possess a tenacious commitment to excellence and an unflagging dedication to the success of each student.

Earlier you were asked to find out if your prospective student leaders just wanted to be called "leaders" or did they want to do the things a leader does. Now ask yourself the same question. Do you want to do the things a leader does? Terry Pearce put it this way: "Remember that there are many people who think they want to be matadors, only to find themselves in the ring with two thousand pounds of bull bearing down on them, and then discover that what they really wanted was to wear tight pants and hear the crowd roar."[3]

Structure

Effective leaders are like architects, engineers, and carpenters all in one. They are adept at designing and maintaining classroom and rehearsal routines within which students can flourish. They construct and repair bridges to learning for their students using their toolboxes of artistry and attitude. They are not afraid to roll up their sleeves and get sweaty working to improve instructional design and implementation. They are not hesitant to tear down or refurbish a routine that has proven ineffective in leading students to learn. But above all, as leaders they are most interested in building student achievement in creativity and performance, and in helping their students become substantial contributing members of society.

Character

John Maxwell writes,

> Whenever you lead people, it's as if they consent to take a journey with you. The way that trip is going to turn out is predicted by our character. With good character, the longer the trip is, the better it seems. But if your character is flawed, the longer the trip is, the worse it gets. Why? Because no one enjoys spending time with someone he doesn't trust.[4]

As a teacher, the white-hot spotlight of student attention will be focused on your character every day. To be effective in leading your students, you must regularly work to develop and exhibit useful habits of character. One way is to own your mistakes. In the classroom, your leadership and positive connection with the students can only be strengthened if, for example, you immediately admit your mistake in misnaming an instrument or flubbing a passage on the piano. In conducting ensembles, if you lose your place in the score, stop the group, own up to it, and go on. A typical ploy in this situation is for the conductor to stop the group and point out a problem for the ensemble to fix and then start up again. There has never been a student in all of recorded history that has fallen for that gambit. Students will respect you if you respect them and own your honest mistakes. Respect breeds respect.

Applications of Character

Consider leadership and the component of character in the following scenario. You and the students have established the rule that if a student misses a dress rehearsal for any reason, except for a dire emergency, that student is not allowed to play the concert. You have consistently enforced that rule in the past but you are tempted to make an exception when your principal clarinetist broke the rule. You rationalize the exception by thinking that you are taking into consideration the good of the entire group. How can the concert go on without the first chair clarinet? However, if you demonstrate character by the fair and consistent application of the rule, you will provide your students with a powerful lesson, and you will gain their trust. You also might find that the rest of the first clarinet section will rise to the challenge and perform extraordinarily well. However, it is not the performance that matters; it is the life lesson that is learned by your students as a result of your decision.

Additional tests of your character can occur on overnight school trips. Situations that are part of these events hold potential for leadership character damage. Some teachers leave their character home when they travel with their ensembles; however, effective leaders realize how susceptible they are on these occasions, and they act appropriately. A good rule to follow on such trips is to avoid any hint of impropriety, because even a small indiscretion can become a large issue by the time the story gets passed along to the parents and school administrators back home. As an effective leader, character counts and will have an effect on your students that will influence their lives and the lives of all those with whom they come in contact for years to come.

Character and Trust

No matter where you look in studying about leadership you will find such words as *honesty* and *integrity* used to describe the essential teaching and leadership component of character. These traits point to *trust*, which is the bedrock of leadership. As John C. Maxwell states in *The 21 Irrefutable Laws of Leadership*, "Character makes trust possible. And trust makes leadership possible."[5] Maxwell asks, "How important is trust for a leader? It is *the most important thing*. Trust is the foundation of leadership. It is the glue that holds an organization together. Leaders cannot repeatedly break trust with people and continue to influence them. It just doesn't happen."[6]

In writing about leadership and trust in directing ensembles, Ramona M. Wis comments,

> Once trust is established, accountability can legitimately take place. The ensemble that does not meet the conductor's high standards and clear expectations should be held accountable in a professional way. This means honestly telling students: "This is not your best work. We could accept it, but you and I know it's not your best. You deserve to do better, and I'm here to help you get there. What do we need to do to make this better?"[7]

Character and Faith

In the matter of faith, effective music teachers are not required to check their worldviews at the school door just because they are informed by religion. If your faith defines who you are, it could provide richness and purpose to your philosophy of teaching and learning. Surely the tenets of your faith could function as a positive part of how you act with your students. Faith is often based on goodness, decency, respect, honor, and integrity, and effective music teachers should certainly have those elements as part of their teaching philosophy. If your faith is important to you, you are not expected to suddenly become someone else upon entering a school classroom. Your faith and beliefs should enable you to be more accommodating and respectful to other views, positions, and practices. Remember to consider your beliefs, faith, and worldview as you engage in the process of forming your philosophy of music, discussed in a later chapter.

Characteristics of Leadership from Research

James M. Kouzes and Barry Z. Posner have conducted research over many years on characteristics of admired leaders. They have found "that four qualities have continuously received an average of over 60 percent of the votes. Before anyone is going to willingly follow you—or any other leader— he or she wants to know that you are *honest, forward-looking, inspiring,* and *competent.*"[8] Kouzes and Posner write,

> Being honest means telling the truth and having ethical principles and clear standards by which you live. People need to believe that your character and integrity are solid. They need to believe that you are worthy of their trust. . . . Being forward-looking means having a sense of direction and a concern for the future of the organization. Whether it's called a vision, a mission, or a personal agenda, the message is clear: You must know where you're going if you expect others to willingly join you on the journey. . . . Being inspiring means sharing the genuine enthusiasm, excitement, and energy you have about the exciting possibilities ahead. People expect you to be positive, upbeat, and optimistic. . . . Being competent refers to your track record and your ability to get things done. People have to believe that you know what you are talking about and that you know what you are doing.[9]

These four characteristics connect strongly with the six components of effective teaching. *Honesty* connects with the component "character." Are you truthful in all things? Does your behavior reflect your words—do you walk your talk? Do students trust you?

Being *forward-looking*, or having vision, connects with "communication," "dedication," "structure," and "comprehension." Are you able to cast a vision together with your students and communicate to them the possibilities for success? Are you dedicated to doing whatever it takes to help all students progress as far as possible? How will you work with your students to structure a plan for success? Will you consistently check for student comprehension and use the results to propel progress in this plan?

Inspiring connects with "communication" and "dedication." Are you willing to persevere in helping your students find their own motivation to achieve the vision you and they share?

Competent connects with "content." Do you have the command of subject matter and mastery of methods that will enable you to skillfully guide your students to maximize their potential?

Case Studies of Effective Leadership

To see how these characteristics of effective leaders play out in real life, let's examine what three proven leaders have to say about their success in bringing together individuals to achieve common goals. As you read their comments and the examples of leadership they provide, you will find that they possess the four characteristics cited by Kouzes and Posner (honest, forward-looking, inspiring, and competent).

These leaders also have consistently demonstrated excellence in the six components of effective teaching (content, communication, comprehension, dedication, structure, and character). Above all, you will find that they have "trust" as the foundation for all of their actions. These teachers/servant leaders have been highly effective in leading students, teachers, and organizations as well as developing student leaders at all levels. In reviewing their remarks, think about how you would define leadership, and how you will put into practice those essential characteristics of effective leadership that they highlight.

Case Study: Professor of Music

The first leader we meet is Nancy K. Klein, Ph.D., who is a professor in the Department of Music, Old Dominion University, Norfolk, Virginia, where she is graduate program director and director of choral activities. Her career includes public school service as an elementary and middle school classroom, choral, and instrumental music teacher. At the university level she teaches graduate and undergraduate courses in music education and applied conducting. She also directs a variety of university choral ensembles. Klein has been honored with awards that reflect her effective leadership and commitment to the success of each of her students.[10]

Klein sees effective leadership as the process of getting other people fully and willingly committed to a specific course of action in order to meet an agreed upon goal. Her leadership style might vary depending upon the setting. With a choral performing group she is more of a visionary leader whose style contains three parts:

1. Casting a vision for the music, the concert, and the performance.
2. Communicating that vision to the singers using verbal and nonverbal approaches. Klein explains,

   > You can have a lot of ideas of what you want to do and where you want to go, but you have to be able and willing to communicate those ideas effectively to the group. You have to be able to communicate in such a way that people comprehend what it is you want

to do and what their part of that goal is, then you can help them to learn how to meet that goal.

3. Inspiring the group to reach the goal or achieve the vision (the ultimate performance).

To provide inspiration and achieve the vision, Klein emphasizes the key element of experience. "It's hard to lead people to places you haven't gone yourself. That's why experience is so important."

In the classroom Klein uses more of a transformational leadership model, transforming, through teacher example, the students' perspectives, abilities, focus, and approach to the subject at hand.

The Aim of Effective Leadership

Klein states that "the ultimate aim of effective leadership boils down to helping others achieve their personal best to attain a specific goal," but she is quick to say that "in education there is much more than just meeting the goal that's agreed upon. There is the end result, but there is also the process." She wants to see students grow, achieve their personal best while helping them reach the goal, but she also wants to see them transformed in the process of reaching that goal. She believes that the process is more important than the product. Klein is committed to setting high performance goals for each student that are realistic, or else the process of attaining them will become frustrating.

Characteristics of an Effective Leader

Klein describes five characteristics of the effective leader:

1. *Communication and the ability to inspire people.*
2. *Integrity.* She states, "Without honesty and trustworthiness no one will follow you. People won't follow someone they can't trust. It's imperative that people see what you do is consistent with who you really are." (This is the same point made by Kouzes and Posner, discussed previously in this chapter.)
3. *Strategic thinking* (there has to be a level of critical thinking and problem-solving ability in order to be successful as a leader). In this area, Klein emphasizes the importance of staying calm, finding out what is going on, looking beyond immediate distractions, and coming up with solutions.
4. *Optimism undergirded with awareness of reality.* Klein states, "You are going to face problems especially when going in a new direction. You can't become bitter or frustrated. Even if the outcome isn't what you

thought it was going to be. You have to think 'This is worth my time. This is worth my energy.'"

5. *High level of skill, training, and knowledge or ability in one's content area.* But Klein also points out that "it doesn't help to be knowledgeable if you can't communicate what you know."

In sum, she explains, "These five characteristics apply to leading any age group; however, it is critically important to always keep in mind the importance of developing in each student the ability to function as an independent learner." She warns, though, that leadership can go astray if some performing groups get so wrapped up in a particular director that they don't know how to make music without that particular person. She maintains that "the goal should be musical independence so a student can make music under the leadership of any number of directors."

Students' Descriptions: Leadership and Teaching

Each semester at colleges and universities, students complete anonymous evaluations of their professors. Over the years, Klein's university students have been consistent in their descriptions of her effectiveness as a teacher-leader. They describe her as follows:

- *Excellent communicator*: The students realize that she makes sure that they fully understand where the instruction is headed and how they can get there.
- *Enthusiastic*: She looks at each part of each course as something to really get excited about.
- *Passionate about the subject*: She feels that everything being studied is of the utmost importance and energizing.
- *Caring*: The students have reported that Klein cares about them as people and that she will do whatever it takes to lead them to be successful.
- *Dependable*: Her evaluations also note her ability to build trust. She emphasizes that "students have to know that you are there for them, and that you will be consistent in doing what you say you'll do."
- *Knowledgeable*: Students also say that she knows her subject well; however, she consistently tells them, "There will always be someone who is more knowledgeable. So even though a thorough grasp of knowledge is important, you should never reach a point where you stop learning."

Developing Student Leaders

Klein throughout her career has developed student leaders. In teaching elementary classroom music she would routinely divide her classes into groups for projects, appoint leaders who then chose assistant leaders. That put students in leadership positions right away. With a middle school band she had section leaders, but she made sure that the students knew what their leadership position meant, and what the specific responsibilities were that accompanied the position.

As a middle school chorus teacher, she was able to develop leaders through the planning, preparation, and performances that went along with a trip to Washington, DC, where her students sang on the Capitol steps and performed for members of Congress. She and her students together planned the itinerary, set fundraising goals, decided on music, and voted on many decisions. She reports that "the trip proved to be a life changing experience for those students many of whom had never traveled anywhere, even in their own state. Four of those students went on to become public school music teachers where they were able to cast visions for others."

At the university level, as someone who trains prospective teachers in the classroom or in rehearsals Klein sets up an environment to force every student to think critically. She describes what she is doing and why it should be effective. She requires students to assess the effectiveness of a rehearsal approach, assignment, or project. She is constantly communicating about the "what," "where," and "why" of whatever is attempted in class. Her goal is "to prepare future teachers to think through problems, analyze solutions and learn how to inspire their future students to want to learn."

With the university choral ensembles, she develops leaders by having the students gain ownership of whatever group they are in by constantly asking them to analyze their singing and make musical decisions. She also develops leaders through the use of choir officers, section leaders, and student conductors. Klein regularly uses music education majors to run sectionals and assist in planning performances to give them some experience in musical and nonmusical problem solving.

At the graduate level, she develops leadership skills in graduate assistants by helping them as they assume teaching duties at the undergraduate level. She maintains, "The best way to develop student leaders is to model effective leadership skills, characteristics and traits continually. Much of leadership ability is learned by watching those who are effective at it."

A Leadership Challenge

Because the university choral program had outgrown its performance space, Klein knew that she had to find another venue, so she improvised a concert hall in a large atrium in the fine and performing arts building. Because the space was used for other nonmusical events, there were built in problems with scheduling, seating, and acoustics. But the choirs had to have somewhere to perform, so she worked closely with other departments and the university facilities people to make it all happen. It wasn't easy because nothing like this had ever been done before, but she was determined to succeed.

She reports, "I had to roll up my sleeves and work along with the students in creating a workable performance space. Persistence paid off so well that now other music ensembles have followed my lead and regularly use the space."

Klein cast a vision for her singers of how this would work, and they supported, helped, and followed the project through. Both Klein and her students learned that the keys to success in this project were persistence, problem solving, and the ability to stay focused on the ultimate goal.

The Reward of Leadership

Klein comments, "In everything I do, I am constantly reminded that the authentic reward of leadership is in watching the growth and transformation of those you are leading as they attain agreed-upon goals."

Case Study: Public School District Director

The next leader exemplifies effective teaching and leadership. James J. Cassara is former director of music education for the Northport–East Northport Union Free School District, Northport, New York, and director of fine arts and music education for the Connetquot Central School District on Long Island, New York. His teaching career includes directing pit orchestras and concert, jazz, and marching bands at the elementary, junior, and senior high school levels. Cassara is former president of the New York State School Music Association (NYSSMA), from which he received the Distinguished Service Award. Currently, he is student-teacher supervisor for Long Island University.[11]

We now take a look at leadership at work with staff and students in the public schools through Cassara's extensive experience as a teacher and administrator.

What Is Leadership?

Cassara characterizes leadership as "the ability to gather together individuals having various personalities, abilities, strengths, weaknesses and viewpoints, to create an atmosphere in which the individuals work as a group with unity of purpose to reach a common goal." He puts this description to work through his leadership style, which includes a great deal of listening to the views of the teaching staff, encouraging open discussion, and being a facilitator in assisting them to reach a common goal. He emphasizes, "The common goal should always center on the question, 'What's in the best interest of the students?'"

His style also features leading by example. Cassara states, "I would never ask any member of my staff to do anything that I wouldn't do." He cites the annual marching band citrus sale, where he always assisted in unloading the trucks and checking out the student orders. He also enjoyed participating in the annual faculty recitals and announcing every football halftime performance.

Cassara states, "In all aspects of leadership we must keep the focus on the success of the students, and work to ensure that all students are given the opportunity to receive a well-rounded education that includes a comprehensive, sequential, high-quality program of music." To do this, he targets the following characteristics of an effective leader:

- *Be a good listener*: Staff and students must trust that their opinions will be heard and that initiative will be encouraged and supported.
- *Be honest*: All staff and students must be treated fairly and honestly. A good leader never lies. Provide an honest answer to the best of your ability.
- *Be decisive*: After gathering all the facts regarding an issue, make a decision. Every decision should be based on the bottom line: "What's in the best interest of the students?"
- *Be visible*: The leader makes himself or herself visible to the entire community and demonstrates that he or she is approachable. Staff and students must know that the office door is always open and that you are available.
- *Be loyal*: Cassara maintains, "An effective leader is loyal to the staff and is viewed as the spokesperson to the greater school community. As a leader, the staff needs your public support balanced with private, professional, constructive criticism."

In each of these characteristics, we see Cassara as a fine example of a servant leader who truly puts the success of others ahead of personal success and achievement. His staff validates this view. They describe his leadership as "honest, supportive, perceptive, and organized."

Student Leaders

Throughout his career Cassara developed student leaders through building a strong Tri-M National Music Honor Society that brought together students from every aspect of the music program. As the department head, he took a hands-on approach by becoming the chapter advisor. This approach allowed him to build rapport with the students as they met and developed performance opportunities, community service, and the unification of the entire music department.

These Tri-M students developed as true servant leaders. They chose not to have official officers; rather, Cassara and his students all worked together as a team. Whenever a recital, fundraiser, or other event was planned, it became the work of the whole group. Natural leaders emerged and took responsibility for every aspect of the activity.

Cassara also built leaders by involving students in hiring teachers to direct ensembles. He had every prospective teacher candidate conduct a performing group as part of the interview process. Then he met with the students to listen to their impressions of each candidate and included that in the decision-making process.

At Tri-M meetings, students frequently took the initiative in suggesting events and ways to improve the music program. "A number of these initiatives were of merit and received my fullest support. This support was a clear demonstration to the student leaders that they could take an active role in shaping the organization, and thereby encouraged their continued input and creativity in planning future events," Cassara explains.

Leadership and Learning

Cassara views the effective leader as one who supports and facilitates instruction, and never loses sight of the value of combining leadership and learning. As an example of combining leadership, support, and learning, his high school orchestra director came to him, as department head, with the idea of performing Prokoviev's "Peter and the Wolf" for all of the second- and third-grade students from the entire district. Cassara offered to narrate the piece and arrange for the students to be brought to the high school. Each of the district classroom music teachers taught a unit on program music using "Peter and the Wolf" to educate the students who would attend the daytime concert. The performance was repeated in the evening for the community, and afterward the Tri-M students served more than eight hundred ice cream sundaes to the audience. That project certainly combined leadership and learning.

The Future

For the twenty-first century and beyond, Cassara's views on music education leadership and effective music teaching include the hope that educators in all subject areas truly believe in the necessity of music study for a complete education for all students.

"We don't teach music for math's sake, we teach music for music's sake. Instead of stating that smart students study music, my hope is that parents, students, all teachers, and administrators will understand the message 'Music makes students smarter,'" Cassara emphasizes.

Case Study: Music Education Administrator

The final case study for leadership in music education focuses on Steven E. Schopp, Ed.D., who is executive director of NYSSMA, Westbury, New York. Schopp is former music and art department chairman for the Syosset Central School District, Syosset, New York, and has served as president of the Eastern Division of the Music Educators National Conference and NYSSMA. Over the course of his teaching career Schopp directed concert, jazz, marching, and show bands, as well as orchestras at the elementary, junior, and senior high school levels. He has taught college music education courses, and currently supervises student teachers from Ithaca College, Ithaca, New York. He has been honored by awards that attest to his leadership ability and record of success. Schopp's wide and deep experience provides us with a valuable and useful model for effective leadership.

Leadership Essentials

Schopp views leadership in the light of inspiration and ownership. He states, "Leaders inspire people to follow, even in ways they didn't want to go or know they wanted to go. It's difficult to really make anyone do anything. They have to buy into an idea, that is have some ownership, to really be effective."

As an effective servant leader, he leads by example. As a department chairman and executive director, his leadership is characterized by his own level of professional activity that he trusts will be emulated by those who serve with him. He maintains, "In all of my leadership roles, I rarely told people they must do anything, but I always made it clear what I wanted them to do." His leadership is fueled by the hope that those he leads will become self-motivated and committed to a common goal. To be effective, Schopp is convinced that the most important characteristics of an effective leader are initiative, integrity, enthusiasm, energy, optimism, and persistence. He comments, "Persistence might be even more important than the other characteristics."[12]

Student Leaders

In his role as a public school music education leader, Schopp used the high school music department's Tri-M chapter as the primary vehicle to develop student leaders. The chapter was designated International Chapter of the Year more than once, and was mostly student run. Schopp's approach was to guide students, but let them make the major decisions and then expect them to be responsible for implementation. For example, any request from the community for special small-ensemble performances went through Tri-M. The officers returned calls, assigned performing groups, and were responsible for being sure the groups arrived and performed as promised. Schopp approved such performances and helped as needed, but the students had a lot of power, which resulted in ownership of the process.

"If the ultimate goal of education is to guide students to be independent (and I think it is), then leading students into situations, guiding them, and then getting out of the way is the ultimate hands-on learning experience," he emphasizes.

His Tri-M officers were not simply elected by the group or chosen by the teachers. Each year, those who were interested in being an officer had to apply, and a panel of current officers, with an advisor sitting in, interviewed each candidate. And the interviews were tough! For example, "You're already an officer in three school clubs, how do you think you have time for this? This isn't just another line on your college application, is it?" Being an officer was never a popularity contest, and the officers were real workers and leaders.

Schopp firmly believes this real sort of responsibility and independence is the key to building student leaders. He built this sort of leader by using the Tri-M students to run a NYSSMA festival. He needed students to work the office, and he needed commitment for the entire weekend if the contest grades were to be recorded accurately. He called in the Tri-M president and told her what the expectations were. He let her choose her crew, but suggested that she find the most meticulous students she could. To emphasize the importance of scrupulous attention to detail, Schopp told her about a scenario where a student's grade was posted incorrectly as an "A" when it later turned out to be a "B." She turned white at the thought, and he knew she would get the message across to her fellow workers. He reports, "I had given her the job and I allowed her to do it with little interference. I knew she was in charge when I arrived the next morning and she was already on the phone telling her crew to arrive on time (something that would have been inappropriate for *me* to do). Tri-M worked well—that year and every year thereafter."

Schopp reinforces the goal of building effective student leaders by stating, "The whole purpose of the learning process is to develop individuals who can function on their own. When they do this, they lead. As students learn, their teachers and mentors must back away and let them lead themselves. To lead others you must first lead yourself!"

A Leadership Challenge

Early in his leadership as district department chairman, Schopp saw the value of increased levels of student participation in the NYSSMA festivals and activities. He reasoned that students who prepared for the festivals worked harder, practiced more, took more lessons, and even bought better instruments, regardless of the outcome of the festival. He thought that even if a student became ill the day before the festival and missed it, he or she had still gained from the preparation, and the more students who participated, the better the department and the ensembles would become within the program. He started with an initial district-wide NYSSMA participation level of two hundred to three hundred students and a few all-state students each year. His vision, though, was for many more students to participate. Along with that vision he also knew he could not require teachers to send their students or mandate that they be enthusiastic about it. That is not Schopp's servant-leader style. So, he set an effective example by being active and enthusiastic himself. He became very involved in local and state activities and made sure his staff knew how much he appreciated their activity as well. They always saw him at the festivals and at their performances. This was a long-term endeavor and required commitment and persistence. But others followed and picked up the ball.

As a result of leading by example, Schopp reports,

> Our 200 to 300 participants grew to 1,200 to 1,300, and double-digit all-state numbers became the norm. Many assumed that it was because our students had more access to private lessons, better instruments, or whatever, but that really wasn't the reason at all. Our students did well because they gained confidence from their teachers and they saw their peers having success. Their teachers went the extra mile in their preparation, coaching them, fitting solos to the students, and matching them with the right accompanist.

Through his example, NYSSMA participation became the norm—the thing to do without much prodding from the teachers. Schopp states, "I've always believed that the hardest task is to get the very first student into All-State (or whatever select group). After that, the other students will think, 'He or she is a good performer, but I could do that!' And so they do."

The Future

Schopp is optimistic about music education in the twenty-first century, even in this age of worshiping statistics, data, and standardized test scores. He believes that an education in music enables students to see the world differently and to express themselves in ways others can't begin to understand. He is convinced that there is a critical need for leaders at all levels that appreciate this and who can, and will, express it effectively. Schopp observes that music teachers now have incredible technology at their disposal while still having, and needing, all the traditional instruments. He sees that the possibilities are endless if all music educators can be creative enough to develop them.

Music educators have always been required to advocate for music education and have actually been rather effective at doing so. Schopp looks at this advocacy and the future by stating, "If I have a hope, it would be for a society that gains an appreciation of the value of music and the arts so that more time can be spent making music and less on advocating for it. My expectation, however, is that advocacy will remain as necessary as it has been since Lowell Mason took on the Boston School Board."

Summary

Each of these leaders emphasizes the combination of artistry and attitude that results in effective teaching. They are consistent in their use of leadership descriptors such as content knowledge, communication, integrity, optimism, enthusiasm, energy, and persistence. These are precisely some of the same words used to describe effective teaching. These leaders also demonstrate the critical importance of developing student leaders by providing opportunities for students to plan, make decisions, take responsibility, and function on their own. It is clear that the three leaders cited here demonstrate by their actions that they truly are servant leaders who place the good of the group ahead of personal gain, build trust, and who are committed to developing student leaders who do likewise.

Above all, these leaders recognize that without trust, leadership is impossible. They reinforce the need for mutual trust between leader and learner that is based on an optimistic view of human possibility. All three cite integrity, honesty, and trustworthiness as indispensible for effective leadership. In the first case study, Nancy Klein sums it up by stating, "Without honesty and trustworthiness no one will follow you. People won't follow someone they can't trust. It's imperative that people see what you do is consistent with who you really are."

As you continue to develop your own leadership style, reflect on the example set by these veteran leaders and think how you will use their experience to enhance your progress in becoming an effective teacher–servant leader. In all, you and your students can enjoy possibilities for growth and success if you emulate the traits exhibited by these leaders, build a trusting relationship, and believe in the limitless potential for each of your students.

John W. Gardner in *On Leadership* speaks of this belief and potential:

> If one is leading, teaching, dealing with young people or engaged in any other activity that involves influencing, directing, guiding, helping or nurturing, the whole tone of the relationship is conditioned by one's faith in human possibilities. That is the generative element, the source of the current that gives life to the relationship. William James pointed out that just as our

courage is so often a reflection of another's courage, so our faith is often in someone else's faith.

When the faith is present in the leader, it communicates itself to followers with powerful effect. *In the conventional mode people want to know whether the followers believe in the leader; a more searching question is whether the leader believes in the followers.* [italics in the original][13]

For Reflection, Discussion, Assignment

1. Using the leadership case studies in this chapter as examples, interview a school leader (administrator or teacher), and provide a one-page summary of the interview. Seek responses to the following: What are the characteristics of an effective leader? How do you develop student leaders? Name a leadership challenge you have faced and describe how you overcame it. What can hinder effective leadership? Be prepared to discuss the interview responses and how the leader's answers align with the six components of effective teaching: content, communication, comprehension, dedication, structure, and character.
2. Review one journal article or newspaper article about leadership from any field. Discuss what the source reveals about leadership and how the results could be used or avoided in your teaching.
3. Think about the leaders in your life that have been successful in helping you grow as a student and a person. Identify and be prepared to discuss at least three attributes of leadership that one of these leaders has demonstrated.
4. Name any leadership positions you have held. Discuss any problems you faced and provide examples of how you solved them.
5. Identify any problems you encountered as a leader that you were not able to solve. Explain your attempts to solve these problems and why you think you failed.
6. Articulate the type of leader you hope to be. Supply two specific scenarios that would typify your leadership.

Resources

Battisti, Frank L. "Teaching Music: The Leadership Component." *Music Educators Journal* 85, no. 6 (May 1999): 38–41.

Block, Debbie Galante. "Tri-M Society Helps Leaders Flourish with Student-Run Programs." *Teaching Music* 16, no. 3 (November 2008): 58.

Farr, Steven. *Teaching as Leadership: The Highly Effective Teacher's Guide to Closing the Achievement Gap.* Hoboken, NJ: John Wiley and Sons, 2010.

Gardner, John W. *On Leadership.* New York: Free Press, 1990.

Greenleaf, Robert K. *Servant Leadership.* Mahwah, NJ: Paulist Press, 2002.

Kouzes, James M., and Barry Z. Posner. *The Truth about Leadership*. San Francisco, CA: Jossey-Bass, 2010.

Maxwell, John C. *The 21 Irrefutable Laws of Leadership*, 10th ed. Nashville, TN: Thomas Nelson, 2007.

Raessler, Kenneth. *Aspiring to Excel: Leadership Initiatives for Music Educators*. Chicago: GIA, 2004.

Rudaitis, Cheryl. "From Student Leaders to Leading Teachers." *Teaching Music* 3, no. 4 (February 1996): 40–41.

Wis, Ramona M. "The Conductor as Servant-Leader." *Music Educators Journal* 89, no. 2 (July 2002): 17–23.

7

Forming Your Personal Philosophy of Music Education: What Do You Believe Is Important in Teaching and Learning Music?

This chapter contains a process to enable you to develop a practical, personal philosophy of music education and statement of teaching. By engaging in this process, I hope that you will learn more about yourself and what you believe is really important in your day-to-day teaching. You will be asked to reflect upon the information contained in previous chapters and identify areas for improvement. You will also be asked why you want to teach music, how your attitude will affect your teaching, and how all of this connects with the six components of effective teaching. You will then proceed to combine your answers to these questions and articulate your thoughts in a two- or three-page written personal statement through which the reader can picture you in action in your classroom or rehearsal situation.

Linda K. Thompson makes the observation that in music teacher training programs, instructors "often find that students articulate a wide range of viewpoints, shedding light on who they are, their images of teaching and learning, and their perspectives on the profession. Yet often we do not appropriately acknowledge these beliefs, nor do we usually assist our students in recognizing, making explicit, and examining their beliefs."[1]

Whether you realize it or not you already have a system of beliefs that operates in your life. Lynn Cooper writes,

> We all make many decisions every day, and those decisions are based on what we know and believe. In other words, our daily decisions are based on our "philosophy." Many of us have not taken time to actually write out a statement that summarizes our beliefs about a certain topic, but we do already have a belief system in place because of our educational training, our personal experience, and our conscious or unconscious deliberations about that topic.[2]

For effective teaching, it is essential that you take these beliefs and connect them with the art of teaching and learning. Your beliefs should form the foundation for everything you do throughout your teaching career. Reflecting upon and articulating your beliefs must be done before spending any time trying to implement lesson plans at the front lines of teaching. Trying to plan what the goals are for your students is difficult, if not impossible, if you do not know what you believe. If you base your lessons on what you deeply believe, your teaching will be honest. If you teach what you believe, students will more likely to be swept along to success by your teaching artistry and attitude.

It makes sense that a thoughtful, personal statement of teaching and learning should be formed early in your professional development. It is much like having the sound you desire from your performing group already in your ears before and during the rehearsal, or like having goals and the pathway to achieve those goals thought out in advance of teaching your general music students. This is not to say that your philosophy, desired sound, or goals will never change, but without a foundation of beliefs that directs your teaching, your day-to-day interaction with the students will lack focus, and you could fail to help students make as much progress as might otherwise be possible.

As you start thinking about building a personal philosophy of teaching and learning, ask yourself, "Why teach music?" "What are my personal beliefs about how to teach music?" "What do I believe is important in teaching and learning music?" Veteran and new music educators as well as college music students would assuredly provide a variety of answers to these questions. Yet all might agree that what you personally believe about teaching and learning can substantially affect your teaching success. Constructing a philosophy of music education based on your beliefs will provide you with a special opportunity for self-reflection and professional growth. Armed with a well-thought-out personal philosophy of teaching and learning, you will be more confident in your planning and delivery of instruction. Your statement can also provide clarity of thought and response as you advocate for your program with parents, administrators, community members, and various organizations. Having a clearly defined philosophy of teaching and learning will certainly help you articulate the importance of music education if your area is facing cutbacks, or if you are asked to make a curriculum presentation at a Board of Education meeting, or if you are speaking with parents at a Back to School night. With few exceptions, you will find that parents, administrators, students, and teachers in other disciplines will respect your role in developing the whole child if you are able to speak clearly and intelligently about the why, what, and how of teaching music. In addition, your written philosophy of music education is an essential part of the professional portfolio that you will present at job interviews.

Students' Thoughts about What Music Means

To provide some inspiration and get you thinking about why you are devoting your professional life to teaching music, review the following comments written by public middle school chorus students. Their teacher became interested in what her students thought about music, and what music meant to them. To find out what they thought, she asked them to complete the statement "Music is . . ."

As your philosophy of music education evolves, it could prove useful for you to keep in mind what these students wrote from the heart. It might be useful for you also to finish the phrase "Music is . . ." What is music to *you*? The eighth-grade students responded with the following comments:

"Music is a release for me. It is like painting a picture, you need tools and paint. The brush is our voice. The paint is our imagination and the blank canvas is the world for our minds to leave our mark on forever."

"Music is inspirational. It inspires everyday life and experiences. Music stimulates the senses and gets people thinking. It connects the world with one common bond—passion. Whether you speak the same language or not, all people can understand the language of music. It takes us to another world where there is no war or hate, only the common love for music. Connections with other cultures are few but music is strong and powerful and can unite people forever. Music is inspiration."

"Music is all around us. It is unique. It gives us the ability to express things we can't put into words. I am music and music is me."

"Music is a treasure, something that you hold onto for the rest of your life. Treasures, however, are only for people who treasure them. You see, treasures are full of promise, and promises, just like music, are to keep and to share."

"Music is my life. I live for music. I think God put me on earth to make music. Music is elegant and beautiful. If you like a certain type of music, it can show your personality. The way music sounds can show feelings. Music calms me down and puts the world aside."

"Music is something that breaks you down, brings you up, and brings you down again. Music can turn a dull life into a joyful life. Music is a place of serenity, a place of freedom. We get inspired by music! We listen to a rap song and now everything seems different. Music changes lives, and other thoughts we may have. Music is irreplaceable. The world would not go on without it. So in all, music is like my own piece of heaven."

"Music is a sunny day in a meadow full of wildflowers and sunflowers. Music is the rainbow in the sky after the horrible rain. Music is the morning bird's lovely lullaby that wakes you up after a good night's sleep. Notice how all these things are as lovely and wonderful as the music we hear everywhere. It is not just a song or melody, it's something much deeper. Only you can determine the deepness and many details of music. I think music is not just a line of notes but a valley full of musical desire and meaning. Music is a mixture of instrumental, rock, pop, country, hip-hop, R&B, and more. All of these kinds of music come together and form a bowl of happiness. In conclusion, music is a very special thing."

"Music is a second language to me. If you speak English, French, Spanish, or any other language you can still escape into music. You can use music to show a feeling, ask questions, get answers, or just enjoy it. Music is something I love and always will. It's something I understand and cherish. To me, music is knowledge of a lifetime. It's not like school. It's not a pain to learn. I cherish it. It's music!"

"Music is everywhere. It has been used for a long time, ever since God created the earth, actually. I may do other things, but I will always turn to music if I need help, if I need to express myself or anything like that. Music has always been and always will be the best thing on earth!"

Keep these student comments in mind throughout the process of forming your philosophy of music education. These powerful personal statements reveal what music can mean to each child. In establishing your beliefs about teaching and learning music, focus on how the study of music can act as an essential component in educating for creative literacy.

Your Beliefs about Teaching Music

Recall what you wrote at the very beginning of this book about (1) why you believe it is important and necessary for all students to study music, (2) what you identified as traits of the effective music teacher, (3) what you want your students to learn, and (4) how you are going to help them learn those things. As a class or in small groups, review those responses and discuss to what degree, if any, your ideas have changed about teaching and learning music. Write down any changes to what you wrote before. This exercise will assist you as you go through the following process in constructing your personal philosophy of music education.

With all of the published ideas about music education philosophy, writing such a statement might seem daunting; however, if the process is broken down into a few sequential areas of reflection, you might find it easier than you think.

You will begin by answering some basic questions and forming your responses into three lists: (1) reasons why you teach music, (2) attributes of attitude in how you teach music, and (3) six components of effective teaching. These lists will serve as a strong foundation for a practical, productive statement of the way you function as a music teacher at any level, in the classroom or rehearsal space.

The "Why" of Teaching and Learning

Why teach music? Do we teach music to build self-esteem and teamwork? Do we teach music in order to improve scores in math, languages, and science? What makes music study particularly special and necessary?

If you focus on the unique, inherent qualities of music itself, you will be on strong philosophical ground. In forming your list of reasons why you teach music, review the following standards provided by MENC: The National Association for Music Education, and think about how they affect why you want to teach music:

1. Singing, alone and with others, a varied repertoire of music
2. Performing on instruments, alone and with others, a varied repertoire of music
3. Improvising melodies, variations, and accompaniments
4. Composing and arranging music within specified guidelines
5. Reading and notating music
6. Listening to, analyzing, and describing music
7. Evaluating music and music performances
8. Understanding relationships between music, the other arts, and disciplines outside the arts
9. Understanding music in relation to history and culture

Now answer the following questions by yourself or discuss them as a class: Other than for its intrinsic worth, why do we study music? What makes music a separate art form and intelligence? In what special ways does music enable us to communicate? How does music connect us with other arts and cultures? How does music help us transmit cultural heritages?

After reflecting on these standards and questions, think about what you believe to be most important in learning music. Identify three reasons why you teach music.

Why I Teach Music

I believe that music study is special and necessary because:

1.

2.

3.

Once you have completed your list of reasons for teaching music, add meaning to the "why" of teaching music and make it applicable to the teaching-learning process by asking yourself, "Now that I know why music study is special and necessary, what effect will I have on students and their learning? How will I teach?" Use the following process to form your second list based on what you believe is the most important attributes of attitude in how you teach.

The "How" of Teaching and Learning Music

Attributes of Attitude

Remember the high school seniors from the In Honor of Excellence event mentioned in chapter 4? Those seniors chose three teachers (one each from elementary school, middle school, and high school) who had the most influence on their life and learning. Like them, think about the most important teacher in your life, that one person who had a profound influence on your life and learning. What were some specific teaching traits that made that teacher special? Reflect on those traits and how that teacher used them in causing you to learn. Will you use similar characteristics in your teaching? Keep these in mind as you construct your second list.

Use the ABCs of attitude from chapter 4 in forming your second list that delineates attributes of attitude in how you intend to teach. Out of the twenty-six ABCs of attitude, choose six to eight attributes that are your favorites, those that you believe best describe you and how you intend to teach. These attributes should resonate with the way you think and act. They should align with what you believe is most important in teaching and learning.

Using the ABCs of attitude from chapter 4, list your six to eight choices here:

1.

2.

3.

4.

5.

6.

7.

8.

You have developed two lists: (1) why you teach music and (2) attributes of attitude in how you teach. For your third and final list, use the six components of effective teaching, discussed in the following section, and arrange them in an order of importance that reflects your personal beliefs about these components of effective teaching. Your list does not have to follow a straight line of importance from top to bottom. For example, if you believe some of the components are of equal in importance, you might want to place them side by side. Or if you think that one component is of the highest importance and all the others link to this one area, you might want to create a wheel arrangement that places that component in a hub position with the other components forming spokes.

Six Components of Effective Teaching

Review the following six components and arrange them in priority order of importance. Use a list or create a diagram to show their relative importance according to your beliefs.

1. Content
   - Mastering subject and technical skills
   - Knowing high-quality literature and materials
2. Communication
   - Exhibiting cooperation and understanding
   - Displaying a natural sense of humor
   - Knowing ways to create a positive learning atmosphere
   - Knowing how to lead students to learn how to learn
   - Involving all students in gaining ownership of what they are studying
   - Addressing student needs by knowing a variety of teaching strategies
   - Connecting with all components of the students' constituent network
3. Comprehension
   - Setting high standards and giving students the tools to meet or surpass them
   - Knowing how to measure student achievement accurately and usefully
   - Using student outcomes to measure your teaching effectiveness
4. Dedication
   - To the success of all types of students
   - To excellence and academic rigor
   - To your own professional growth

5. Structure
   - Consistency
   - Planning and preparation
   - Organization and management (people and paper)
6. Character
   - Trust and respect
   - Reasonableness and fairness
   - Ethics and values
   - Honor and integrity
   - Walking your talk

Putting It All Together: Constructing Your Philosophy of Music Education

You should now have three lists: (1) why you teach music, (2) attributes of attitude in how you teach, and (3) a priority listing or diagram of the six components of effective teaching. Using these three lists, think about (1) the "why" of your teaching and learning, (2) the "how" of your teaching and learning, and (3) the relative importance of the six components. Begin constructing your philosophy of teaching and learning by starting with the implied "I believe," and then describe (1) why you teach music, (2) your attributes of attitude in how you teach, (3) your beliefs about the components of effective teaching and learning, and (4) how you are going to put your beliefs into practice.

Outline and Rough Draft

Start by writing an outline that addresses the four areas noted previously. Using this outline, create a rough draft by putting your outline into narrative form. At this stage, don't worry about producing a refined statement. Even though your final statement should be no more than two or three pages, for this rough draft go ahead and write any number of pages to get your thinking flowing.

Second Draft

Now go back and refine your statement, making sure that your thoughts and writing reflect your personal beliefs. You will find that if you restrict yourself to two or three double-spaced pages, your philosophy will have focus and should gain in clarity.

As you further refine your statement, it is very important that your statement provides a clear picture of your teaching. Anyone reading your statement should be able to imagine you interacting with your students in your classroom or rehearsal space. I have read many so-called teaching statements that could have been written by anybody and that could be applied to anyone's teaching. These "boilerplate" philosophies are of limited use in helping you grow professionally or in guiding your planning and delivery of instruction. Instead, provide a meaningful "photograph" of yourself working with students. You can produce such a picture by providing examples from situations you anticipate encountering. For example, you might explain ways in which you would deal with a fifth-grade boy who refuses to participate in any activity that involves singing, or how you intend to connect with students and parents whose first language is not English. You might also include an example of how you hope to teach students with diverse learning needs—for example, how you would respond to a child without sight who wants to be in your band, chorus, or orchestra. Keep your statement focused, and avoid going off topic by writing about the status of music education in the United States, or by providing a polemic for restoring music programs. As important as those areas are, you want to keep the focus on your beliefs about interacting with students.

Final Draft

For your final draft, proofread your statement to eliminate grammatical and spelling errors. Don't depend on a computer program to check your grammar or spelling. It is very helpful to have someone else proofread your statement to make sure what you wrote is logical, easily understood, and free of mistakes.

Once you have your statement written and have applied it to your teaching, it will be a worthwhile exercise to review, reflect on, and revise your philosophy at least once a year, perhaps at the end of each summer as you are preparing to start school.

Conclusion

Through reflection and research, and by examining your personal beliefs about teaching and learning, I trust that your personal philosophy of music education will have strong roots and productive, practical applications. Above all, your philosophical statement should always be in progress—a living document. As you grow professionally, so should your philosophy.

You might be surprised at the results of your reflection. You could find out that you have very definite and special reasons for teaching, and that you intend to use your positive attitude, along with your knowledge and skill to influence the lives of countless young people who in turn will influence others. What a legacy you will leave!

Sample Philosophies of Music Education

What follows are examples of philosophies of music education written by an undergraduate music education student, a student teacher, and a veteran music teacher. Take some time to review these philosophies to see what they think is most important in teaching and learning music, and how they intend to go about leading their students to learn. In reading their philosophies, do you get a clear picture of them working with students? Consider how your philosophy might contrast with or complement each.

Sample Philosophy 1

Undergraduate Music Education Major Alyssa
(Philosophy of Music Education)

I feel that the ancient Greeks had the best philosophy of music. To them music was the study of relationships between hidden objects, the invisible and internal. In today's world, I believe the study of music is special and necessary because it teaches students how to connect the invisible and internal: their minds, bodies, and souls all at the same time. In accomplishing this, music brings together all cultures with a language that everyone can understand, to experience the past and present in real time.

There are many different attributes that make a good teacher. The attributes that I feel are most important are thorough preparation, use of high-quality literature, and relating objectives to students' interests and needs. As a teacher I will always be prepared with complete lesson plans, a classroom that is set up and organized, and an understanding of my students' needs. I will select literature of the highest caliber that allows the students to experience new techniques to expand their learning. I will relate my lesson plan objectives to my students' needs by making sure that they are not learning music that is too advanced for them and at the same time is not too easy. I will also value the opinions of my students and incorporate music that they suggest, by finding arrangements that are of the highest quality.

The important areas of teaching and learning could be combined into six components. These components are content, communication, comprehension, dedication, structure, and character. All of these components are indispensable. I feel that dedication, character, and communication should be blocked together because they encompass ethics and values. As a teacher, I will be dedicated to my school community. I will show this through the actions of my character and communicate this through my instructional techniques. Content and comprehension also go hand in hand because mastery of subject matter cannot be accomplished without assessment. Structure is an essential tool to keep the students involved and focused.

I will apply these beliefs to my teaching every day. I will make sure that my students are exposed to the literature of the "greats" by having them play them and actively listen to them via professional recordings. I will assess my students daily by asking questions such as "What do you think can be done to improve this passage?" and "Where do you think the climax of this piece is?" so that I will keep track of their progress and find out if my curriculum is meeting their needs. Most importantly, I will create an environment that is accepting, where students are not afraid to make and learn from their mistakes. My students will be empowered to express themselves because that is what music is all about.

(Used by permission of Alyssa Montchal.)

Sample Philosophy 2

Music Education Student Teacher Keith
(Philosophy of Music Education)

I believe music education should be a vital part of every child's life. Music gives new meaning to life, and reaches out to all who hear it. Children have the right to be taught the joys that music can bring. Music has an inexplicable power to reach past language, race, sex, and age lines to touch all who hear and learn it. With a musical education, students gain so much more than the aesthetic values observed at first glance. Music allows students to grow as people, and provides a learning environment unlike any other.

Music is a valuable asset to any educational program. Through music programs, students of all ages and backgrounds are given the chance to join in creating something wonderful together. As a music educator I feel it is my responsibility to guide all students to achieve their personal best and to never accept being subpar. I also feel I should be an example to each student I teach. In me, students will find a source of diligence and reliability. In my teaching I will always be honest with students, and provide them with all the assistance I can in every situation. While being honest, I will also always remember to be kind and sensitive with my words. Students need to be pushed to be their best while still being nurtured as they develop their abilities. Nothing is more detrimental to a student's learning than a teacher who expects too much but provides too little. I believe as a teacher it is my responsibility to help students achieve all that music has to offer. My greatest hope, and goal, is that my students walk away from my classroom understanding the major part music can play in their lives, and possessing the resources to continue their musical study if they desire.

As a teacher, I will ensure my students have the ability to learn on many different levels. While the main source of learning will be ensemble playing, students should be exposed to many musical experiences. By exposing students to various musical styles and cultures I hope to broaden their horizons. Technique and skill are important; however, these are far from the only important criteria in music education. It is my goal to leave no child behind no matter the playing ability. Music is a gift that all can enjoy, and should never be withheld due to modest talent.

My hope is that every student I teach will find in me a director who is strict but fair, demanding but nurturing. Through the teaching of music I hope to open children's minds to the world around them and help them see how large an effect music can have on their lives.

(Used by permission of Keith J. Smith.)

Sample Philosophy 3

Veteran Public School Music Teacher Sara
(Philosophy of Music Education)

I believe that music is a vital part of education because it strengthens core subject principles and gives students a creative way to use their imagination. Music allows students to combine their learning experiences because it covers history, science, math, and languages. It is also an important outlet for highly emotional and dramatic students. Music bridges many learning gaps and brings out the best qualities in my students and me. I strive for those moments when a student finally masters a concept, and you can see that "Oh-now-I-get-it!" light bulb of comprehension go off above her head.

I believe that my most important teaching qualities are my passion for music and my compassion for my students. My students know that I care for more than just their achievement in my class; I care about their overall success. I teach with a lot of energy, enthusiasm, and demonstration. For example, when my students don't keep up with the beat and play too slowly, I walk around the room in slow motion. Not only does it make the students laugh, it is also a better reminder to watch the conductor than if I simply stopped and said, "Please watch me." I try very hard to make learning fun. I play lots of games with my students, which tricks them into learning some of the less exciting concepts. For example, to teach different rhythms, we play the human measures game where the students become the notes. By playing such games students really remember concepts.

To be an effective teacher, I am creative. I have more than one way to teach a concept because all students do not learn the same way. I try to relate what is happening in the music with what is happening in the students' lives. When we study waltzes, I make everyone dance. I talk about how waltzes used to be popular party music much like club music is today. Then, every time we play a waltz, the students remember the components of a waltz.

I also believe that to be an effective teacher I have to know my own character and help my students develop their characters. I tell my students if you respect me, I will respect you, and if I respect you, you will respect me. As a teacher, I have to be a role model for my students. Many only see violence and hardship outside of school. I try to make them better people through my actions and examples. My students need to know that I am here to teach because it is what I love. I have a high level of dedication not only to music, but also to their individual successes. I often tell struggling students how I struggled as a beginner and overcame my obstacles. I try to be very encouraging and supportive of my students and all their endeavors, whether music related or not.

I believe that having an open line of communication with students, teachers, parents and administrators is vitally important. Students need to feel that they can come and talk to me when they have a problem in my class. Parents need to feel comfortable approaching me with concerns. When I keep the administration up to date on what is happening in my classroom, they are supportive of my program.

I use common sense, especially when it comes to structure. For example, I have organized all my classroom materials, such as rosin and cleaning cloths, to be accessible to my students and to me. I use classroom time for teaching and learning, not searching for materials.

I teach music by incorporating core subject knowledge, passion, creativity, character building, and communication. I also make learning fun and give my students an attitude that says, "You can do it." I not only show them how to do something but also tell them why they should do it. For example, if they know why it is important to shift while playing, then they are more willing to practice shifting. I tell my students that it is okay if they do not grasp a technique the first time I introduce it; there is always the next time. I also tell my students that just like we play different instruments, we each move at our own pace. But if we support and respect each other, and focus on learning the music, we will become an orchestra.

(Used by permission of Sara Jordan.)

Seeking Knowledge

As you prepare to lead students to learn, and seek to know and grow through the study and performance of music, it is appropriate to let Plato, in his *Dialogues*, have the last word in this chapter on philosophy.

> Socrates: And I, Meno, like what I am saying. Some things I have said of which I am not altogether confident. But that we shall be better and braver and less helpless if we think that we ought to inquire, than we should have

been if we indulged in the idle fancy that there was no knowing and no use in seeking to know what we do not know—that is a theme upon which I am ready to fight, in work and deed, to the utmost of my power.[3]

Resources

Abeles, Harold F., Charles R. Hoffer, and Robert H. Klotman. *Foundations of Music Education,* 2nd ed. New York: Schirmer, 1996.

Campbell, Patricia Shehan, and Carol Scott Kassner. *Music in Childhood,* 3rd ed. New York: Schirmer, 2009.

Cooper, Lynn G. *Teaching Band and Orchestra: Methods and Materials.* Chicago: GIA, 2004.

Elliott, David J. *Music Matters: A New Philosophy of Music Education.* New York: Oxford University Press, 1995.

———, ed. *Praxial Music Education: Reflections and Dialogues.* New York: Oxford University Press, 2005.

Enloe, Loraine. "Your Philosophy Revisited." *National Band Association Journal* 49, no. 2 (December 2008): 35–37.

Grant, Joe W., and Lynn E. Drafall. "Teacher Effectiveness Research: A Review and Comparison." *Bulletin of the Council for Research in Music Education,* no. 108 (Spring 1991): 31–48.

Reimer, Bennett. *A Philosophy of Music Education,* 3rd ed. Upper Saddle River, NJ: Prentice Hall, 2003.

Roth, John K., ed. *Inspiring Teaching: Carnegie Professors of the Year Speak.* Bolton, MA: Anker, 1997.

Thompson, Linda K. "Considering Beliefs in Learning to Teach Music." *Music Educators Journal* 93 (January 2007): 30–35.

8

Case Studies: Artistry and Attitude in Action

John Corigliano is one of America's most eminent composers. His works have been performed all over the world by leading soloists, major orchestras, and such large performing institutions as the Chicago Lyric Opera and the Metropolitan Opera in New York. He has won the Pulitzer Prize in Music, the Academy Award for his film score in *The Red Violin*, the Grammy Award for best contemporary composition, and the Grawemeyer Award. He is currently on the composition faculty of the Juilliard School and holds the position of distinguished professor of music at Lehman College, City University of New York; however, it is quite possible that none of this would have happened if it had not been for an effective music teacher.

Corigliano's parents were accomplished musicians. His father was concertmaster of the New York Philharmonic and his mother was a concert pianist. Corigliano attended Midwood High School in Brooklyn, where his self-taught piano proficiency kept him involved with various performing groups. It was during these high school years that he was encouraged to pursue a musical career by Bella Tillis, a music teacher at Midwood High, to whom he later dedicated *Fern Hill* (part I of his evening-length work *A Dylan Thomas Trilogy*). Corigliano relates what a singular influence this teacher had on him:

> She's a wonderful woman, I really love her. She had a big influence on me. She was the first person to really encourage me to go into music, which is one reason I wanted to dedicate *Fern Hill* to her. She really gave me a feeling that I could be a musician and that I had talent. At a time I really needed a lot of reassurance, she was there. She was a very special teacher. I guess everybody's had a teacher that's been very special and changed his life—she's been the one for me.[1]

149

Bella Tillis exhibited the right attitude at the right time for the young Corigliano. Her caring encouragement resulted in a man who never forgot the interest she had in him as a real person with a real need. The world now has a celebrated composer and distinguished professor, who continues to pass along to his students Bella's legacy of effective teaching.

Case Studies of Effective Music Teaching: Students Report

It is likely that each of us has had a teacher who influenced us deeply in positive ways. The three case studies of effective teaching that follow provide real-life examples of how teachers have significantly affected the lives and learning of individuals.

Undergraduate and graduate music education majors and current music teachers were asked to describe one teacher, kindergarten through university level, who had the most influence on their life, learning, and development as a music educator.

Three case studies of effective teaching are presented here that are typical of the descriptions provided. As you read them, think about the characteristics of each teacher and imagine how you would be described, what your teaching motto would be, and how you would combine your content knowledge and methods of instruction with your attributes of attitude. Each case study demonstrates artistry and attitude in action by profiling a teacher who had a significant influence on a particular student's life and learning.

Case Study of Effective Teaching: Mr. G., Orchestra Director

Mr. G.'s teaching is characterized by his compassion for all students, his patience, and an infectious passion for music and learning. His teaching approaches feature a natural sense of humor and creativity. His former student reports, "Mr. G. always began class with a humorous story and he continually showed his love and passion for music by performing for the class." Mr. G. sprinkles his teaching with creative stories to help his students remember concepts, and even dances around the room to provide a picture of the emotion of the piece his students are working on. He often ends class by asking his students about their day and how things are going. His student states, "We mattered to him." This caring attitude permeates his teaching and creates a positive, productive teaching atmosphere. His students know that they mean a lot to him, and because of that they trust and respect his teaching leadership.

"Don't be afraid to play from the heart," is Mr. G.'s motto. He supports this approach by getting his students to perform with passion and understanding through the use of storylines to reflect the structure and expressiveness of each piece of music. He then has his students play as if they were telling that story. His former student relates how Mr. G. has influenced the way she teaches now. "In my own teaching, I try to use creative methods to help my students learn. I use movement, gesture, and imagery to assist the students in capturing the musical essence of pieces we are studying."

Mr. G.'s instructional approaches are effective and creative. For example, he never gives textbook definitions for musical terms. He describes the appropriate effect, or demonstrates it, and then has his students come up with a definition in their own terms that they then apply to the music. Armed with this personalized knowledge his students perform with deeper understanding.

Mr. G. also engages his students by programming music that is of high quality and potentially exciting. His student reports, "Even pieces that could have been boring, Mr. G. made them exciting because he helped us connect with the inner musical meaning of each one." Mr. G. regularly reinforces learning by demonstrating on his main instrument as well as on all of the other instruments. "This inspired us and provided a useful model for us to emulate."

Case Study of Effective Teaching:
Ms. S., Classroom and Chorus Teacher

Ms. S.'s effective teaching features a caring, respectful attitude with each of her students. She has thorough command of her subject content, sets high expectations for all students, and provides them with the tools with which to achieve those expectations. Above all, her day-to-day interaction with each student is characterized by trustworthiness. Her former student states, "Ms. S. expected our best work and was always willing to help us produce it. She was *always* available after school to help you with whatever you needed. We could trust her to always be there for us."

Ms. S. helps her students become independent learners. They learn how to learn because Ms. S. has her students apply clearly articulated concepts and skills to a variety of learning activities, thus providing reinforcement for their understanding. This "transfer of knowledge" approach also gives Ms. S. the opportunity to consistently check for individual student understanding and provide additional help where needed.

Ms. S. gives her students the gift of musical independence by teaching them to sight read. Her student reports, "Ms. S. engaged us in daily sight reading practice and by modeling the elements of diction. Ms. S. used rehearsal time efficiently by establishing a structured opening routine. This practice gave us time to sight read using solfeggio syllables and hand signals. By teaching us how to sight read well, she gave us the necessary tools for musical independence." Ms. S. further reinforces this independence by providing her students with many varied opportunities to perform in small and large ensembles, and in the classroom. "She always gave us a ton of chances to showcase our talents that built our confidence and made us strive to do our very best," her former student remarks.

Together with her special ability to help students learn how to learn, Ms. S.'s teaching style includes the building of character. Her student states, "Ms. S. demonstrated not only effective instructional techniques but she also modeled great character. She made me want to be a better person. She was interested in our overall success not just in our musical achievement. Consequently, I try to do the same in my teaching."

Case Study of Effective Teaching: Mr. A., Chorus Teacher

Mr. A. is a knowledgeable, caring, and talented teacher who is passionate about his subject and is able to motivate all students to do their very best. He exhibits the ability to engender positive attitudes in all his students. Mr. A.'s former student recalls, "His classes were often filled with students who only took the class for what they thought was an easy 'A.' But by the end of the first term, those students came to his class because they loved singing, not just for the grade."

Mr. A. is able to change his students' attitude toward learning music in part by spending many extra hours helping all students realize their potential. His command of content and passion for learning rubs off on each one of his students. He leads several after-school ensembles to encourage students from all parts of the school to make music a part of their lives beyond the classroom. His teaching approaches can be summed up by the motto, "Music is a part of life, not just a part of school."

Mr. A. provides enduring learning by applying concepts through a variety of activities in a range of musical situations. For example, when teaching rhythm, he has his students speak, clap, and move using combinations of rhythm patterns so his students will relate head knowledge to performing. His former student remembers, "Mr. A. was always able to teach material in multiple ways to make sure that all of his students were able to understand what he was presenting."

His student goes on to describe how Mr. A. taught a sixth-grade choir how to breathe effectively for singing. She tells how he spoke plainly to this mixed-ability class without the students feeling that the lesson was dumbed down for their benefit. For the students who learned from hearing information, he explained the process of breathing while he also drew a diagram on the board for the graphic learner. Then he demonstrated proper breathing as it related to producing a supported tone. His former student states, "This was novel information to every student in the class, but I believe that we all came to understand the concept of breathing because of his multiple modes of instruction, even if we weren't able to produce perfect results yet. Even after hearing literally dozens of subsequent lectures on breathing by many qualified instructors, this lesson still proved to be one of the most effective of my life."

Student learning improves because Mr. A. uses varied methods of instruction and presents material in clear, simple terms without a hint of condescension. Students end up wanting to learn as a result of Mr. A.'s caring attitude, content knowledge, and passion for his subject. In addition, his positive influence reaches beyond the music classroom because he involves students from all areas of the school in a variety of small performing ensembles. Many of the students with which he comes in contact end up staying involved with music beyond their school years because of his commitment to make music a part of their lives, not just a part of school.

Summary

Each of these three case studies demonstrates that teacher attitude is the driving force in causing substantive changes in student learning. Lives were changed and learning made enduring because these effective teachers knew their subjects, were passionate about what they were teaching, modeled character, and genuinely cared about each student as a person.

Case Studies from the Front Lines of Teaching: Teachers Report

Additional artistry and attitude in action is here provided by examining two in-service music teachers whose experience represents the first years of music teaching, and many years of public school service. The first case study is of a second-year music teacher. The second case study is of a twenty-four-year veteran. Reflect on how these effective teachers relate to their students, and think about the traits of effective teaching exhibited by the teachers that influenced their lives and learning. What teaching approaches and qualities will you seek to emulate in your teaching?

Case Study: Newer Teacher

Teaching Approaches

Ashley Phillips teaches classroom music, chorus, and orchestra at two K–5 public elementary schools in Norfolk, Virginia.[2] She leads her students to learn by providing manageable portions of content that she introduces and reinforces through a variety of activities. She is always careful not to overload her students with too much information. "In college we dealt with many complex content areas, but I do my best to help the students understand this content without confusing them," Phillips states. She provides her students with the amount of information necessary that will help them understand basic concepts and skills, while consistently working to align the information to her students' achievement and ability levels.

Phillips regularly helps her students understand concepts and skills by putting them within a performance context. This approach allows her to model the content on her cello. She notes, "Having played a musical instrument for the past fourteen years, I recognize this experience as one of my strong points. I am able to transfer those years of performing over to my students who are usually just beginning to learn different ways to study music." Phillips combines modeling and what she has learned through her performance experiences, to lead students to learn through classroom discussions, demonstrations, and hands-on activities.

Structure

Phillips's effective teaching is enhanced by her attention to planning and organization. She states, "I believe structure is a core element in ensuring success when teaching, because, as the saying goes, 'If you fail to plan, you plan to fail.'" Her organizational skills are bolstered by her high degree of personal musicianship and content knowledge, and she connects these skills to her students by reminding them that once she was also a beginning music student in a city school just like theirs, so she understands their situation and lets them know she will help them achieve their dreams. She states, "When they observe all of the knowledge that I possess and my musical abilities, the students become motivated to push themselves even further."

Style

Phillips's teaching demeanor is characterized by kindness, care, and a natural sense of humor. She reports, "My teaching style is very calm and approachable, which makes it easier for students to participate who may normally shy away from performance activities." She sets high goals for them to achieve, and her students understand that she expects nothing other than greatness from them. She mentors a number of her students outside of the music setting, and she finds that they respond positively to her enthusiasm and high expectations in all learning situations. She notes, "While still maintaining a strict classroom management structure, I am able to allow my sense of humor to make learning music fun and entertaining."

Mentor and Model

Phillips cites one teacher who served as her mentor and model for teaching effectiveness. Mr. Marc Haas from Cass Technical High School in Detroit, Michigan, had the most influence on Phillips's life and learning. She reports, "Mr. Haas is dedicated, caring, knowledgeable, determined, inspiring, and humorous. I owe any success I have had or will have in teaching to his encouragement and nurturing ways." Phillips explains that Haas approached her during her junior year in high school and stated that she possessed the "knowledge and kind nature" that are essential elements in being a success as a teacher. She relates, "Mr. Hass reminded me that there would be ups and downs during my teaching career, but that I could always find motivation in seeing students grow through participation and dedication."

This highly influential teacher encouraged Phillips and all of his students by sharing stories of his satisfaction with making music, and what he learned when he was in school. He faithfully stays in touch with his students. As Phillips states, "His support for me certainly did not stop once I left high school." Throughout her teacher training and her first two years as a music teacher, Phillips has always been motivated by her mentor's motto: "Never give up!"

New Teacher Challenges

As a new teacher, Phillips dealt with various challenges. During her first year of teaching, she had to deal with students who were adjusting to having a new music teacher after having one teacher for many years and another for just a brief period. At first, some of her students were resistant to connecting with her teaching approaches and exhibited behavior problems because they were not ready for change. She states, "To help smooth the transition, I continued to maintain a calm and fun teaching style, while placing emphasis on my content knowledge." She reports that this strategy reassured the students that they would still be able to learn many concepts in music while having an enjoyable experience at the same time.

She tells of another challenge she faced as a brand new teacher that involved putting together her very first concert program. Phillips notes, "Because holiday performances are a huge factor in elementary schools and require a great amount of planning and practice, I knew that program planning would be one of my most daunting tasks of the school year." Fortunately, her district has a superb new-teacher mentoring program, so she was provided with ample support and the resources to overcome any obstacles that presented themselves. She states, "I combined this support with my planning and organizational skills to create effective programs."

Another challenge she faced and overcame involved a student who was very nervous about singing a solo in front of the chorus class for the first time. The student came to her privately and told her that she was excited to sing for the class; however, she was very nervous and scared about what reaction she would receive. Phillips spoke with the student about what songs she liked to listen to and talked with her about building confidence in performing by using her family as a small, friendly audience. The student agreed to go home and practice singing in front of her family. During this talk Phillips also reminded her of how outgoing she had proven to be in the past (this was sometimes a behavior issue), and how she could channel this energy and confidence into solo singing. Phillips reports, "On the morning of her solo, she greeted me excitedly saying that she had a surprise song that she learned from her aunt to use for her solo. When it came time to sing, she closed her eyes, and released a tremendously beautiful sound. She blew us away!" After finishing her song, the student received much praise from her classmates, and admitted that she should not have been so nervous in the first place. This was a very rewarding and enlightening experience for teacher and students alike.

The Future

In the coming years, Phillips hopes to see music education in the United States at an all-time high. As the economy improves, she envisions more focus being placed back on the arts and less on job elimination. She hopes school districts across the country will be able to reinstate previously cut positions. Phillips holds out hope that all students will be able to participate in cultural enrichment activities without any worries about funding for participation or transportation, and she is optimistic that with increased funding, states will be able to welcome back elementary string programs, after-school music programs, and free or low-cost private instruction for all students who want to learn.

As she develops as a music educator, Phillips sees herself becoming increasingly adept at helping students learn. She is confident that she will be successful during her probationary years and that she will become an increasingly effective teacher. She plans to continue to improve her classroom-management techniques, and develop a variety of strategies and approaches to facilitate delivery of instruction. She states, "I hope that as a result of my teaching my students will gain a lifelong love of music and learning in general."

Case Study: Veteran Music Teacher

Frank C. Garcia is a music teacher and arts administrator at the Visual and Performing Arts Academy housed at Salem High School, Virginia Beach,

Virginia. Garcia is a veteran teacher with twenty-four years of public school experience.[3] He has been honored with many awards that not only recognize his achievements in music teaching but also honor his exceptional contributions as an educator of distinction for all students.[4] For example, at his current high school he is the lead mentor for all students in all subjects.

Garcia believes that he received these awards because he is a lifelong learner who is passionate about the art of music and teaching. He maintains, "I'm a positive person, I place student needs as a first priority, and I try to remain current in the profession in using best practices as well as following recent trends both as a musician and as an educator. Also, I am a competent performer and a fair and consistent teacher."

Knowing the "Good"

Garcia leads his students to learn by having command of content and mastery of methods. He is effective in guiding his students because he knows what "good" is, and is committed to the lifelong pursuit of teaching, learning, and performing. He observes that there are a lot of successful music teachers who are not very strong musicians and a lot of strong musicians who are not very successful teachers. But the best music teachers are the ones who are able to master the art and also are able to become master teachers. In knowing what "good" is, he asserts, "If the ensemble you're directing is really the best musical experience that you've had, I think you're shortchanging your students, because you're just along for the ride rather than leading the way."

Artistry and Attitude

In all his teaching, Garcia effectively combines artistry (content knowledge and skills, personal musicianship, teaching methods) with attributes of attitude such as caring, humor, commitment to excellence, and enthusiasm. He states, "My students tease me because I'm always happy when I'm in the classroom. I'm always positive no matter how bad things are going. My students often comment that I know where we're headed, I am positive about getting there, and that I enjoy what I'm doing, so I hope that attitude carries over to my students."

Garcia wants to be "checked in" as part of the teaching-learning process. He uses the expression "checked in" to mean one who is committed and involved, and one who perseveres and knows what's going on. He wants to be the first one at school and the last one out always. His students imitate this example of dedication. Garcia's commitment to his art is evident. He comments, "I have a healthy respect for our art and its importance in our lives. It's not a hobby for me and I don't want music to be just a hobby for my students. I want it to be a course of study that continues beyond their school years. The students feel that and respond well."

Garcia feels an obligation to expose students to a range of experiences that connects them to the broader arts scene. He states, "They might say 'I like what I know.' But my job is to be the initiator, to expand what they know by involving them in such things as going to professional performances." For example, he sponsors an opera club that goes to performances at the professional opera house in the area. At first, the students were reluctant to get involved, but after the first few trips the word got out that the experience was different and enjoyable, so now students flock to sign up for the event.

Garcia is also "checked in" to the success of students outside the music area. He emphasizes, "I make sure I serve on committees that deal with all school issues not just the music program. As school lead mentor I work with students from all subject areas, so I consider myself an educator in the comprehensive sense of being involved with all aspects of the school." This inclusive attitude is a testament to Garcia's dedication, and provides him with increased opportunities in communicating with all types of students.

That One Special Teacher

Garcia's life, learning, and teaching were most influenced by Dennis Zeisler, who is director of bands at Old Dominion University in Norfolk, Virginia. Garcia comments, "I've known Dennis as a mentor and teacher for over thirty years. He is a master teacher, a virtuoso musician, a top-shelf conductor, fine administrator, and a great communicator. He's dedicated, devoted, and honest."

Garcia particularly notes Zeisler's ability to match his teaching approaches to each student's personality. Garcia relates,

> My brother and I both had Dennis as a teacher. I thrive on having my feet held to the fire. I want opinions about my work straight and blunt. Dennis used that approach with me. My brother is a very different kind of guy. He's the kind of student who receives information, criticism, and motivation differently. Dennis was able to motivate my brother effectively by matching his teaching to my brother's personality. I use that same approach in my teaching.

Over the years Garcia has come to realize that he is teaching individuals rather than the group. He comments that Zeisler provided a model for that mindset, and was able to make a difference in the lives of many people. Garcia notes that he is a more effective teacher because he follows the example set by Zeisler in being involved in his students' lives, and by always being interested in each student as a person.

Dennis maintains that involvement beyond the student years. I know of many, many other people who have had him, and they have had the same experience. He never stops mentoring and giving freely of his time and expertise. From the time I was his student to now as a colleague, he always demonstrated genuine respect for me as a person that made me feel good about what I was trying to accomplish.

Music Education and a Changing World

Garcia notes that life in general has changed. He cites the difficulties students face when thinking about what's important. He states, "Band, orchestra, chorus, and ROTC used to be the only electives; now the amount and types of courses offered even at the middle school level are many, and that takes away from involvement in the performing ensembles."

Overall, he sees technology as having made the biggest difference in the world. He comments, "When I started teaching we were a paper-and-pencil society; now we're in the age of information with social networks, school websites, etc." Garcia acknowledges the effects of this whole new world, and notes that music educators have to keep up with what's out there, and find ways to interact usefully with technology.

Garcia cites two additional areas that affect music education—high-stakes testing and the changing family. He remarks, "High-stakes testing in a range of subject areas has taken away time and shifted the emphasis away from the arts, and the world has gotten more complicated for families." He notes that teachers have had to become more responsible for parental-type tasks because society has given up a lot that used to be the family's responsibility. These additional responsibilities have changed the role of all teachers considerably.

Teacher-Preparation Programs

Garcia hopes that teacher-preparation programs would include emphasis on how to advocate for music in the schools, because as time goes along it will get harder to maintain music education as an integral part of the school curriculum. He asserts that teacher-preparation programs must also prepare students to be effective in teaching students of other cultures because of the increasing diversity of the student body.

Prospective teachers must be taught the nuts and bolts of the profession so they are not surprised if they are the ones to set up the band chairs and stands, put up the choir risers, or perform a million other down-to-earth tasks. Prospective music teachers should be strong musicians, but also know how to deal with these sorts of everyday, practical issues.

Above all, Garcia maintains that if preservice music teachers want to be effective, they have to work on their communication skills. He states, "You can have the greatest stick technique in the world, sing like an angel, play trumpet like crazy, or be a great cellist, but if you can't make it work in the school you're in and connect with the students you have, that's a problem."

Summary

You have read of the influence of a high school chorus teacher on a budding composer who needed encouraging, and you have read of others who have influenced the lives and learning of current music teachers. You have heard a newer music teacher and a veteran educator offer their views on artistry, attitude, and a variety of topics. Second-year music teacher Ashley Phillips cited her mentor's characterization of artistry and attitude as "knowledge and nature." Veteran teacher Frank Garcia referred to this same combination as "knowing what good is" and being "checked in." However it is framed, each of the teachers highlighted in this chapter exhibits characteristics that connect meaningfully with the six components of effective teaching reviewed earlier. Content, communication, comprehension, structure, dedication, and character all come to life through the artistry and attitude of these special teachers. The effectiveness of their teaching will surely extend far beyond their students' school years. The artistry and attitude of music teachers everywhere can combine effectively to lead all students to experience the limitless joy and satisfaction in learning what the art of music offers.

Read what one eighth-grade chorus student eloquently wrote about the power and beauty of this art we teach:

> Music is a huge part of my life. It's so magical. Music can touch you very deeply. I have been singing my whole entire life—to be exact, from when I was two. When my brother was born, I would sing to him every day. His favorite song was "You Are My Sunshine." My mother joined the school chorus when she was my age and stayed until she graduated. I want to follow in her footsteps. Music has changed my life in the best possible way. It has helped me through my toughest struggles and it still does. Music is not just about notes and lyrics. It's about changing people's views on life. A piece of music is like an actual person. The notes and lyrics are like the parts of the body and they tell exactly what is going on. I cannot explain how deeply I am in love with all of the types of music out in this large world. Music will stay in my life forever and I will not let go of it.

To conclude, the distinguished professor Ernest L. Boyer comments on the critical importance and influence of the art of effective teaching:

In the end, inspired teaching keeps the flame of scholarship alive. Almost all successful academics give credit to creative teachers—those mentors who defined their work so compellingly that it became, for them, a lifelong challenge. Without the teaching function, the continuity of knowledge will be broken and the store of human knowledge dangerously diminished.[5]

For Reflection, Discussion, Assignment

1. Complete and be prepared to discuss your own case study of effective teaching using the following the outline.
   - Five characteristics exhibited by the one teacher who had the most influence on my life and learning are _____.
   - The single most effective teaching approach this teacher used to help me learn was _____.
   - This teacher has influenced how I teach or intend to teach music in the schools in the following ways: _____.
   - In one paragraph, describe how this teacher effectively combined mastery of content and methods with delivery of instruction.
   - If this teacher had a motto, it would be _____.
2. Have two preservice or in-service music teachers complete a case study of effective teaching. Compare and contrast the results in a class discussion.
3. Using the case studies from the previous two activities, compare and contrast the results with the effective music traits from the research literatures that appear in chapter 1.
4. Conduct the same interview with a college music professor. Discuss differences and similarities between effective college-level music teaching and effective public school music teaching.

9

Administering Your Program: Nuts and Bolts

The practice of administering your program is built on teacher artistry and attitude combined with all of the six components of effective teaching we have been examining in earlier chapters. This area is extensive, important, and contains many potholes to avoid. By using your growing effectiveness as a teacher in administering your program, you will smooth the path to learning for your students. Without the effective administration of the many practical situations that are part of your job, students will be held back in their learning. For example, learning can be hampered and valuable time will be lost if the literature you are studying is disorganized or incomplete. In the music classroom, if your instruments are missing parts and are in disrepair, the audiovisual equipment is broken, or your piano is out of tune, your students will miss out on satisfying music making.

You might not have an administrator's title, but you will have many, many administrative tasks to perform to make your program run effectively. Your day-to-day journey through the school year and over the summer months will be filled with duties that extend far beyond such structural elements as lesson planning and choosing high-quality materials and literature. Over and over again new teachers report that when they began their jobs, the areas that took them most by surprise were the daily demands of paperwork, procedures, politics, and organizational matters. At times these new teachers reached the point of being overwhelmed. I hope that the information in this chapter will help you be more aware of what these demands are and how to handle them.

Punctuality

As you arrive at school ready to teach, you have already gathered your materials, prepared your lesson plans, and groomed yourself to reflect the licensed professional you are. But did you arrive on time? Time management, especially punctuality, seems like such a minor thing, yet inattention to it can affect you in crippling ways. We begin with punctuality because it affects everything else that you do all day long. The following is an extreme example, but it does speak directly to your attitude in this very important area.

Consider this scenario. Your band rehearsal is scheduled to start at 9:14 a.m. You enter the room at 9:18 because your watch is slow. You find the students in an uproar because a fight had occurred in the instrument storage room just before you arrived. Two students are injured. You get the situation under control and try to find out what had happened. Medical personnel must be called, a police report filed, administration and parents notified, and an accident/incident report has to be completed. At the bottom of the report is the line that says, "Teacher in charge at time of incident." You were supposed to be in charge at 9:14 but you were not there. You can imagine the problems that could arise from this situation.

So, if you are the kind of person who is not normally committed to being on time, think about adjusting your routines so you will be punctual. What if you have car trouble or some other emergency? You must immediately call the school so arrangements can be made for coverage of your students because even that tall, imposing senior who has not yet turned eighteen is a minor and must be supervised by an appropriate adult while in school.

Time Management

Effective music teachers make time work for them. They know that if they are punctual and use time efficiently they will have more time to help students succeed. That is why they do not start class or rehearsal with announcements. That practice wastes the most important learning time of the period. Prime learning time is the first minutes of any class. Announcements can be placed on the board. Besides, students will tend to get to class on time, and you will gain valuable instructional minutes, if you start with making music rather than making announcements. Just before you end the rehearsal with a short, satisfying portion of music, one or two special announcements can be made very briefly by a student leader as you double check the attendance. In the general music classroom, engage students right away by having music playing that is connected to the lesson as they enter the room. Music making and learning throughout the entire class time should be your regular practice.

Attendance Procedures

Like the fight scene described previously, taking attendance is another area that has legal ramifications. The attendance register you complete and sign is a legal document that is locked away at the end of each school year and is archived for years. Students are not allowed to take attendance. But what about your 150-member ensemble? Assign seats and make up a chart with a little box for each student. You can then quickly note those students who are absent or late during the "Do Now" portion of the rehearsal. You can double-check the attendance just before the end of the rehearsal during announcement time. For classroom music, incorporate attendance into the lesson by making up an attendance song where students sing their names and answer "present" in call and response fashion. Or have assigned seats and, as with a large ensemble, use a chart with boxes. In all events, know and follow the attendance procedures of the school to the letter. It might sound trivial, but you can save valuable instructional time and avoid legal issues if your teacher attitude includes maintaining a keen sense of the value of time and detail.

Teacher Responsibility

Teaching effectiveness can improve by being proactive in addressing areas that could distract you, hinder instruction, and cause legal problems. It is apparent in what you have read already that much of administering your program falls under the large umbrella of teacher responsibility as applied to all six of the components of effective teaching explored throughout this book. However, administering your program goes even further, for it involves procedures, issues, and challenges that contain potholes but also can produce possibilities for program health and growth. These areas can be addressed successfully by working to increase your knowledge and skill, and by applying what you have learned about teacher attitude and the six components of effective teaching.

Effective music teaching includes the use of efficient procedures that save time, produce important information, align with educational goals, and help provide a safe learning environment for all students.

Trips, Fundraising, Parents

Few areas are as volatile and contain as many potential political issues as those involving taking your students on a trip, handling money, and interacting with parents. The effective music teacher starts by following the most important rule: learn and comply with all school policies and procedures completely and meticulously.

Trips

When considering a trip you must plan well in advance, sometimes a year or more. Some school districts have detailed procedures to follow that include providing complete information about the educational value of the trip, a detailed itinerary, all personnel involved, and all fundraising activities. In some districts, all trips and all fundraising for the entire year must be packaged and presented to the school board by a date soon after school begins in the fall, so "timely planning" should be your motto.

Above all, the trip must be a natural outgrowth of the curriculum. For example, in the chapter on communication, the study of the music of the ancient Mali included a field trip to a local concert hall to hear and see the music and instruments of that culture. If you are planning an ensemble trip, include growth opportunities such as adjudication sessions, workshops, master classes, and visits to historical sites. Consider scheduling performances featuring your group alone, as well as arranging side by side rehearsals or performances with other schools, professional ensembles, or college groups.

As in all aspects of your teaching, keep the administration and parents informed regularly before and during the planning and implementation of any trip. A political pothole to avoid is announcing to your students that they are going on a trip before receiving approval from the administration. If the trip is not approved, you then face disappointed students and parents, and the possible perception by the administration that you used the students and parents as leverage. I am hopeful that you won't fall into that political pothole, and that all your trips will be approved.

You will face critical issues that extend beyond just taking trips. Consider the following four areas that are integrally connected with school trips, but can affect other parts of your program.

Fundraising

Fundraising contains high potential for problems. You must be extra careful any time you deal with fundraising or collecting money for any number of things that your school allows, such as equipment, supplies, travel, materials, uniforms, instrument rental, or even charity. Obviously students can collect money involved with fundraising, but they have to account for every item sold and every penny collected. Other than that, under no circumstances should any student handle money without the direct uninterrupted supervision by approved school personnel. Students should never be involved with making deposits or collecting money from other students.

Here are some sample statements that have often accompanied money issues and students: (1) "Please sign me up for the trip. I will pay you later." (2) "I have almost all of the money from my fundraising. There are still some people who owe me money, but let me settle up because I know today is the deadline." (3) "Please, may I have the trip T-shirt? I will pay you this afternoon." You should answer these questions and others like them by starting with a quiet "I'm sure that you understand: (1) I will sign you up for the trip when you bring in the money. (2) Today is the deadline so we will settle your account today based on what you submit, and please nicely tell the people that still owe you money that you are sorry, but today was the deadline. (3) When you give me the money, you will receive the T-shirt." These responses are fair and consistent and will help students understand the meaning of responsibility.

Keep detailed account books in accordance with school policy, adhere steadfastly to deadlines, and don't bend the rules you have established. Having stated that, there are a very few extreme reasons for exceptions to rules, but make sure the reasons are of the utmost concern and carefully verified. Make sure all of your students will be able to participate in your proposed trip regardless of their financial situation. Some parents will simply write a check; others will need enough fundraising opportunities for their child to pay for the entire trip through those means.

Parents

The school will have definite rules for chaperoning procedures such as the number of chaperones required for the number students participating, but in addition, meet with chaperones and parents (some might be both) early on in the process to review rules and expectations, and to assign specific responsibilities. For example, for an elementary trip you could assign chaperones for the head and rear of lines for specific classes. Others can be in charge of bag lunches, articles of clothing, or any materials and supplies. For a secondary-level trip, you could assign chaperones to head up squads for equipment and instrument loading and setup, uniform or robe teams, and to oversee specific buses. Chaperones and students should be assigned specific seats on buses for attendance purposes, and chaperones should be assigned seats for each bus. Put together information packs for chaperones that detail their responsibilities, and provide school rules and consequences, answers to frequently asked questions, complete trip itinerary, and school contact information. If fellow teachers are chaperones, you should provide them with medical and emergency contact information for each student. Students should also receive similar trip packs, but without personal information about other students such as medical concerns.

Student and Teacher Behavior

A trip can seem like a time away from the rules of the school; however, those rules still apply as you travel. Away from home, some students may feel emboldened to act inappropriately, so your pretrip meetings with chaperones, parents, and students should reinforce expectations. During the trip, be vigilant in enforcing the rules fully. Even in the relaxed nature that can accompany parts of your trip, remember at all times that you are in charge as the licensed professional. You will have fun, of course, but always maintain a distinct line between teacher and student. Avoid even the appearance of impropriety.

Booster Clubs

Often parent-support organizations are involved in trips. They can provide valuable assistance by taking care of a multitude of organizational tasks. These parent groups also can assist in raising money for the trip or other functions and needs. Once again, it is very important to follow school procedures with these clubs.

Meet regularly with the leadership and attend their meetings. You are the school district person who is ultimately in charge of the booster club. If the club starts to work contrary to the ideals and goals of the music program, you have to act quickly to provide leadership and guidance. Sometimes just a private, one-on-one meeting with each leader or various club members can resolve troublesome issues and redirect the group to align with the curriculum and stated mission of the music department. This sort of personal attention can give you the opportunity to answer questions, provide information direct from the horse's mouth (you), and allow individuals to voice their concerns. It is a good idea to be on the agenda of club meetings to answer questions and offer a report on aspects of the music program. This approach takes time, but will pay off because often you can deal with minor issues before they become large problems by clarifying things parents might have heard from other parents or their children.

If the booster club is a club for only part of the program (e.g., the marching band), it would be wise to include in your meeting report other activities of the whole music department and the rest of the band program. This approach helps to maintain and reinforce the concept of a music *department.* Or consider a department-wide booster club that can help broaden support for a larger number of students while preventing territoriality and tunnel vision that might result if a club supports only a single group. A music department could gain advocacy strength from such a unified parent group.

Inventory and Library

There is administrative software available that will help you in many areas of administering your program, but one of the most important areas is keeping track of uniforms, robes, classroom and ensemble instruments, books, equipment, and literature. Your district has invested a lot of money into your program and you will be officially in charge of a wide range of items. For example, even a modest collection of Orff instruments can be worth thousands of dollars. Add to that electronic devices and other instruments, and your inventory could be even more valuable.

Inventory

If your district or building does not have a system for inventory maintenance, you should create your own so that at the beginning and end of each school year you know what you have, where the items are, and to whom they are assigned. For instruments and other equipment, note the make, model, and serial number (if available), purchase date and price (if available), condition, and record of repair. Also document the whereabouts and condition of all other materials such as robes and uniforms.

Part of the inventory process is signing out equipment, instruments, robes, and uniforms for repair or for students to use. Avoid the temptation to give a student a uniform or instrument without documenting it. I know of one extreme case where one student had five baritone horns signed out to him without any record of their return. On paper, that student had many dollars of school property at his home. Commitment to effectiveness in this area is critically important.

Library

The music library could be considered the backbone of the department as it provides a rich range of resources for teaching and learning. Its careful maintenance can save you time and serve as a positive force in your program. Here, too, there are systems and software you can purchase to keep things in order, but you can create your own. For example, in the case of performing ensemble literature, for each group keep a master list of titles with composer, arranger, or author; publisher; level of difficulty; date purchased; cost; vocal or instrumental ranges; genre or style (e.g., march, patriotic, bright swing); special features of the piece; dates performed; performance venue (location, event, awards won); and conductor and ensemble names. Group other materials in alphabetical order by title or author, composer, or arranger under headings such as textbooks, scores, periodicals, reference works, software, audiovisual recordings, solos, and chamber literature.

The care of a library might sound like a relatively easy task; however, it will demand your consistent, regular attention. Your support materials can become a tangled mess very quickly without your constant commitment to keeping detailed records up to date. The assistance provided by student leaders in this area will be most helpful.

To keep track of concert literature, at the end of each performance place boxes at strategic points and train students to deposit their folders into them as they exit the stage. Why not collect the music back in the rehearsal room? You would be surprised at the number of folders that go missing between the auditorium and the rehearsal hall. By the end of the next day, at the latest, all of the folders should be emptied by student leaders, and the music meticulously put back in the library and records updated. Band and orchestra literature must be put back in score order. If you keep on top of library maintenance, you will increase your effectiveness through efficiency.

Ethical and Legal Issues

Copyright

If you photocopy music or other copyrighted material illegally, it is stealing. But what does "illegal" mean for music teachers? There is the common misconception that if the music is copied for educational purposes, it is legal. That is not true. For detailed information about copyright law and music teachers, access the free copyright information that appears at www.menc .org > Resources > Online Publications > *The United States Copyright Law: A Guide for Music Educators.* There you will find a booklet that contains information about a wide range of copyright issues. The booklet provided may be copied legally.

The MENC booklet states the following:

> The intent of the law seems to be that music educators can do several things, without having secured permission of the copyright owner:
>
> 1. Make a copy of a lost part in an emergency, if it is replaced with a purchased part in due course

2. Make one copy per student of up to 10% of a musical work for class study as long as that 10% does not constitute a performable unit
3. Make a single recording of a student performance for study and for the school's archive
4. Make a single recording of aural exercises or tests using copyrighted material
5. Make up to three copies to replace a copy that is damaged, deteriorating, lost, stolen from a public library or archive (or if the existing format has become obsolete, and if, after reasonable effort by the library/archive, an unused replacement cannot be obtained at a fair price)
6. Make one copy of a short verbal or a graphic work for teacher's use in preparation for or during a class

The following, however, are expressly prohibited:

1. Copying to avoid purchase
2. Copying music for any kind of performance (but note the emergency exception above)
3. Copying without including a copyright notice
4. Copying to create anthologies or compilations
5. Reproducing materials designed to be consumable (such as workbooks, standardized tests, and answer sheets)
6. Charging students beyond the actual cost involved in making copies as permitted above

Note that although a work may be out of print it does not mean that permission is given to copy and distribute that work. Music educators sometimes would like to procure a copy or copies of an out-of-print copyrighted work for specific purposes. For that reason, the music publishers' trade associations have prepared a simple form for use in the procurement of out-of-print works.[1]

Private Instruction

Ethical and perhaps legal issues surround teaching your school students privately. Whether you receive any money for the lessons, ask yourself, "Isn't it a conflict of interest if I teach these students privately and then give them a grade in school?" What about the students who do not study privately? If your district has a policy about this issue, be sure to follow it. If there is no such written policy, consult with fellow teachers to find out the common practice of the department and consider that together with your own ethical and moral code.

Professional versus School Performances

To help with questions about professional performances versus school performances, MENC publishes a code of ethics that contains detailed information about the province of professional musicians and the province of school performers. Access this information by going to www.menc.org > Resources > Online Publications > *The Music Code of Ethics.* When in doubt about a possible conflict, this online resource can help clarify matters. A good rule to follow is to avoid performances by your school group that are in conflict with services normally provided by professional musicians. For example, a conflict is leading your official school performance ensemble in providing music for pay for a wedding or bar or bat mitzvah. Those events should feature professional groups. School concerts and other performances such as those for parent-teacher association groups are direct outgrowths of the curriculum and should feature school ensembles.

District and School Policies

Become familiar with the policies and procedures in your district that address such concerns as sexual harassment, recognizing and reporting child abuse and drug use, bullying, taunting, stalking, and student-faculty relations. You must report to the administration any observations you make in these areas and any questionable situations you encounter.

Music department policies and procedures can effectively be provided to the school community via a website that is kept current. The site could contain rules and consequences; curriculum outline with concepts and skills, classroom activities, and current literature; grading policies; expectations for student achievement along with assessment guides; standards addressed; dates of rehearsals and concerts; guidelines for home study and practice; award criteria; policies on cocurricular group participation; audition requirements; and fundraising procedures. Before posting any information, make doubly sure you have approval from the administration and have aligned what you've stated with what your fellow teachers have posted.

Summary

Administering your program efficiently will aid student learning by saving time and addressing issues before they become distracting problems. Strive to hone your administrative skills even if you are not naturally organized; however, if you are a super-structured person, be aware that there will be times that you will not be able to micromanage every single little detail. In all, recall the ABCs of attitude from chapter 4 and realize that your attitude as a teacher-administrator is essential in developing a healthy and productive management approach to your program. By putting in place organizational procedures and practices, you will have more time to spend in contact with your students as you help them achieve success and learn how to learn.

For Reflection, Discussion, Assignment

1. Choose, or be assigned, one source from the following resources and present orally a synopsis of one administrative area covered. Alternatively, choose an article from any source that deals with the organizational nuts and bolts of teaching.
2. Orally present a report on one software resource for administering a school music program.
3. Interview one student teacher or in-service teacher. Ask what organizational strategies or resources they have found to be particularly effective in any two of the following areas: trips, fundraising, parent relations, booster clubs, taking attendance, time management, inventory, library, festivals, competitions, concert preparation and procedures, classroom setup and management. Or ask the student teacher or in-service teacher to comment on effective organizational strategies or resources for any other areas not listed here. Orally present your findings.

Resources

Campbell, Patricia Shehan, and Carol Scott Kassner. *Music in Childhood*, 3rd ed. New York: Schirmer, 2009.

Colwell, Richard J., and Michael Hewitt. *Teaching of Instrumental Music*, 4th ed. Upper Saddle River, NJ: Prentice-Hall, 2010.

Cooper, Lynn G. *Teaching Band and Orchestra: Methods and Materials*. Chicago: GIA, 2004.

Haugland, Susan L. *Crowd Control: Classroom Management and Effective Teaching for Chorus, Band and Orchestra*. Lanham, MD: Rowman & Littlefield/MENC: The National Association for Music Education, 2007.

Maranzo, Robert J., Jana S. Maranzo, and Debra J. Pickering. *Classroom Management That Works: Research-Based Strategies for Every Teacher*. Alexandria, VA: Association for Supervision & Curriculum Development, 2003.

Merrion, Margaret. "Classroom Management for Beginning Music Educators." *Music Educators Journal* 78, no. 2 (October 1991): 53–56.

Moore, Marvelene C. *Classroom Management in General, Choral, and Instrumental Music Programs*. With Angela L. Batey and David M. Royse. Lanham, MD: Rowman & Littlefield Education, 2002.

Rush, Scott. *Habits of a Successful Band Director: Pitfalls and Solutions*. Chicago: GIA, 2006.

Wong, Harry K., and Rosemary T. Wong. *The First Days of School*. Mountain View, CA: Harry K. Wong, 1998.

10

Summary

The Student, Artistry, Attitude, and the Six Components of Effective Teaching

The students you face today are influenced more than ever by competing interests and an uncertain future. They are enmeshed in a market-driven culture and a test-driven educational system. Their communities can accurately be described as techno-global as technology dominates the way they communicate, gather, and use information. Our media-saturated world bombards them aurally and visually for much of their waking hours, and society has seen the role of the family in education continue to change. Are these factors now driving our profession? What fuels your teaching? Who's at the wheel of music education?[1] What should be at the core of your teaching?

Effective Teaching: The Student

Even though you and your students are led in all directions and face an increasingly complex world, your instruction can overcome distraction, stay on track, and gain enduring meaning and purpose if you keep "the student" at the center of all your efforts. Concentrate on combining command of content and mastery of methods with attributes of attitude that will unlock learning for each student. That is effective teaching.

We see in figure 10.1 that the student is placed at the center because each one should be the focus of our profession. Recall the case study of Frank C. Garcia in which he states that thanks to the example set by his mentor, he has come to realize that he is teaching individuals, not the group. This approach is not always easy to keep in mind if you are leading an ensemble; however, Garcia maintains that an important part of effective teaching is

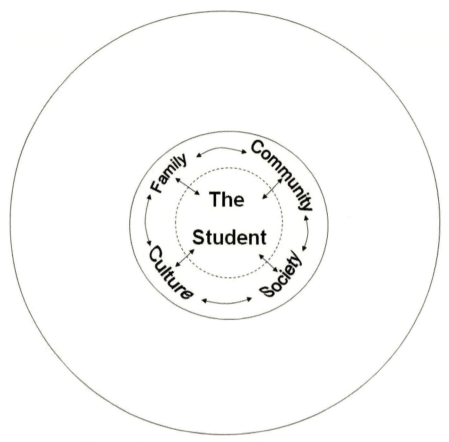

Figure 10.1. Effective Teaching, part 1 (Courtesy of Jonathan Duggan and Erika Mullen)

matching your teaching strategies to each student's personality. By taking that approach the group will benefit. So with the student always at the center of your teaching, you will be less likely to become distracted and derailed.

Figure 10.1 also demonstrates that the units of family, community, culture, and society all influence each other and each student we teach. In turn, the student reflects back these influences, sometimes with change as the student changes. The influence of the family has changed for today's student. More and more schools are taking on responsibilities that have been traditionally shouldered by parents. Cultural traditions are becoming less influential and societal structures are being altered by an uncertain economy, government actions, and global conflicts. "Community" now includes the vast and multilayered world of cyberspace. Social networking on the Internet involves our students in sometimes complicated and distracting ways.

This flow of influences among the units of family, community, culture, and society changes according to the relative strength of each unit combined together with the degree to which each student changes. This flow moves somewhat like liquid in a bowl that is being rocked back and forth by the forces of our time. Sometimes the bowl is rocked violently, as when families and communities fracture or face hardship or when the societal institutions fail and familiar cultural traditions lose their influence. This action can create an overbalance of influence that can drown the other elements and impede learning. However, if the bowl is left untouched, the liquid becomes stagnant, and the flow halts. Effective teaching though moves the bowl enough to balance the influences so the student can learn.

Because family, community, culture, and society encircle and influence the student, it is incumbent upon music teachers to be involved in the total life of each student. Effective music teaching does not just focus on music, but rather the comprehensive education of all students. Remember that earlier you read about connecting with the life of the community, school, and student. You were urged to become a helpful, encouraging part of whatever influences each student. It is certainly important to engage in such practical support as attending athletic contests for your students, but the effective teacher goes beyond that to provide guidance and nurturing to all students in the school. Recall that Frank Garcia is lead mentor for all of the students at his high school, not just the music students. He serves on committees that deal with issues and ideas that include everyone in the school. Teaching effectiveness should extend beyond the music suite. Just as it is important to work together and share goals across the music department among all parts of the program (band, chorus, orchestra, and classroom music), it is also critically important to embrace the education of each student across all disciplines in your school as they interact with the influences of family, community, culture, and society. In taking this approach you will be a true educator, one who educates the total student.

Effective Teaching: Artistry

In figure 10.2 we see the expansion of effective teaching with the addition of teaching artistry. You will notice that the inner rings of the figure are perforated to show that all elements involve and influence each other. Recall that effective teaching artistry contains depth of content knowledge together with facility in delivering instruction (methods). As you seek to grow professionally, your expertise in content and methods will develop to the benefit of your students. Your grasp of content and methods will also affect those units of influence that appear in the outer ring of figure 10.2 (family, community, culture, and society). Your facility in teaching artistry can prevent stagnation by energizing and producing a positive effect on the back-and-forth flow

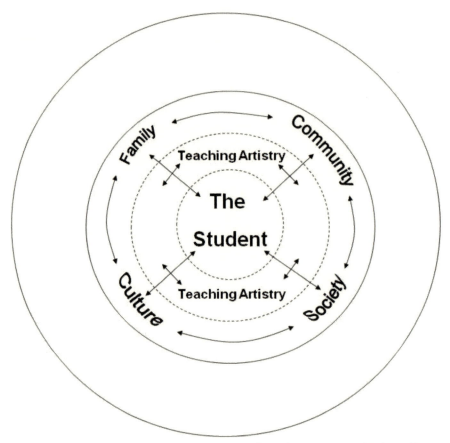

Figure 10.2. Effective Teaching, part 2 (Courtesy of Jonathan Duggan and Erika Mullen)

of influences. Beyond your interaction with the whole school population, it is possible for your music students to have a meaningful effect on family, community, culture, and society as you lead your students to make music and experience its edifying power. Remember the statements made earlier by those eighth-grade chorus students for evidence of this power.

Effective Teaching: Attitude

Next, teaching attitude enters the picture, as shown in figure 10.3. By examining the traits of effective music teaching as revealed by the research literature, and reviewing multiple examples of personal testimony, you have learned that attributes of attitude overwhelmingly affect student learning. Command of content and mastery of methods are essential elements of effective teaching, but teacher attitude is the key that unlocks learning. The

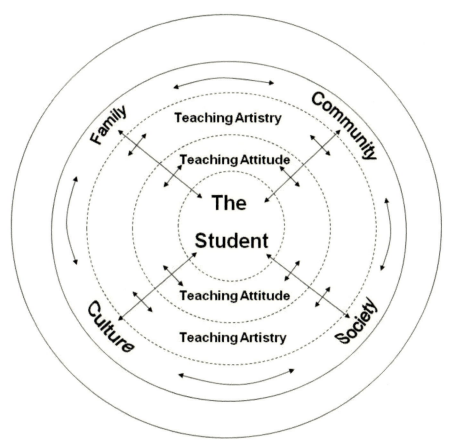

Figure 10.3. Effective Teaching, part 3 (Courtesy of Jonathan Duggan and Erika Mullen)

productive flow of your teaching artistry can be hindered, or even dammed up and stopped if your attitudinal traits are weak, negative, or missing.

Recall the strength and influence of teacher attitude in the life of John Corigliano, and in the lives of Ashley Phillips and Frank Garcia. Remember those high school seniors at the In Honor of Excellence event who honored those special teachers who changed their lives forever. Reflect on how attitudinal traits were prominent in the case studies of effective teaching you read. In all these cases, teacher attitude speaks the loudest. *How* you say something to your students and how you act to support what you say is as important as *what* you say. All students in every subject area that are affected positively by your attitude will be more likely to have similar, positive effects on family, community, culture, and society.

As you consider your attributes of attitude, remember that your teaching attitude will make more of a difference if it is organic, if it is not just applied to your character from the outside but truly comes from inside you—from your heart. Students will sense the integrity of your overall attitude and will be helped in their learning by those attitudinal traits and actions that are genuine.

Six Components of Effective Teaching

Figure 10.4 demonstrates that the six components of effective teaching (content, communication, comprehension, structure, dedication, and character) enter as a force that synthesizes artistry and attitude. These six components bring together the essential elements of effective teaching. All of the characteristics revealed by the research literature and through experience combine in these six components to provide students with the best music education possible. The movement among all of the elements that appear in figure

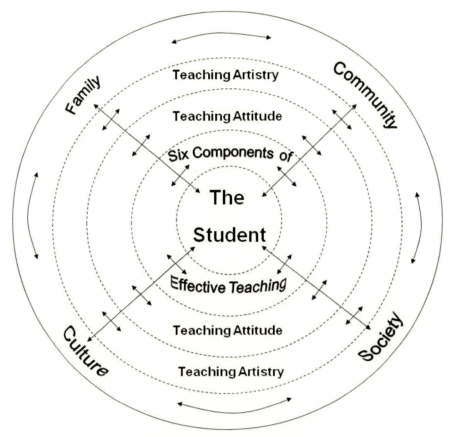

Figure 10.4.   Effective Teaching, part 4 (Courtesy of Jonathan Duggan and Erika Mullen)

10.4 can now be especially productive as they contain the influential flow of artistry and attitude brought together in the six components to result in effective teaching and learning. The four rings of effective teaching as shown in figure 10.4 now just await the touch of the effective teacher to energize the mixture and bring learning to the student.

The Six Components of Effective Teaching

As you read about the six components, think about the degree of development you possess with each one. Reflect on your teaching attributes of attitude and how you will apply them to these components.

Content

- Mastering subject and technical skills
- Knowing high-quality literature and materials

The area of content contains all of your college learning experiences combined with the ongoing development of your knowledge of literature, teaching strategies, and approaches. Your teaching will consist of a mixture of all these things applied to your daily contact with students.

As a licensed professional, you will be somewhat like a physician. You will be called upon to diagnose and provide remedies for individual and group problems in comprehending and executing concepts and skills. If you have a firm grasp of content, you will more likely to diagnose problems accurately and provide remedies that will aid student growth. For example, if you know the acceptable ranges of children's voices as they develop grade to grade, you will be able to choose songs and choral literature that help development rather than hinder it. Learning will be enriched and you will help students more fully understand a variety of concepts if you know a range of musics from various style periods, countries, and genres. If you know what the appropriate sequence of concepts and skills should be as students make progress through the grades, you will be able to enhance learning by matching quality literature to that progress. If you encounter problems in tone quality and intonation, you will be able to provide more effective remedies if you know how the vocal mechanism and instrumental embouchures work, and how students should use their breath and their bodies to produce a quality sound and better intonation. Overall, if you have intimate knowledge of a variety of quality literature that spans the very easy to the more difficult, you will be able to help students grow by matching the appropriate pieces to their achievement levels.

Communication

- Exhibiting cooperation and understanding
- Displaying a natural sense of humor
- Knowing ways to create a positive learning atmosphere
- Knowing how to lead students to learn how to learn
- Involving all students in gaining ownership of what they are studying
- Addressing student needs by knowing a variety of teaching strategies
- Connecting with all components of the students' constituent network

The area of communication contains the "how" of teaching. As has been made clear throughout this book, the power and effect of your teaching depends on how you interact with students to enable the "what" of your teaching to make a difference. A review of the ABCs of attitude from chapter 4 will arm you with a potent arsenal of attitudes as applied to specific teaching situations. As a class exercise, turn back to chapter 4 and identify at least four attributes of attitude that will have a positive effect on each of the bulleted communication items listed previously.

Infusing humor throughout instruction can help maintain student interest and create a more positive learning atmosphere. Your attention to the attributes "nurturing" and "kind" from chapter 4 will also contribute to creating an atmosphere where students feel confident because they have your support.

Having students apply concepts and skills to new situations will provide reinforcement and give you the opportunity to check for individual and group understanding. If you are consistent in engaging your students in this transfer of knowledge and learning, you will be helping them learn how to learn. Regularly involve your students in thinking about what they have been studying or performing, and ask them to offer suggestions for improvement. Students will be more likely to retain concepts and skills and transfer their learning to new situations more effectively if they are invited to gain ownership of the content through their contributions to the instructional process.

It should come as no surprise that using a single teaching strategy with all students will result in uneven achievement levels. Some students will need to see a diagram of the concept you are presenting. Others will need to read a list of concept components. Still others will require hands-on activities to gain lasting understanding. Using a mixture of these strategies will help students learn. With all instruction, you will need to match your strategies to the personality of each student. Some individuals need blunt instructions and a very firm teacher demeanor. Others will need more nuanced directions and a gentler teacher affect.

As was demonstrated in the "Connecting Parents with Learning Project," building connections with families can be an effective way to increase communication. Connecting with all parts of each student's support network is critically important in maintaining open pathways for dialogue and growth.

Comprehension

- Setting high standards and giving students the tools to meet or surpass them
- Knowing how to measure student achievement accurately and usefully
- Using student outcomes to measure your teaching effectiveness

By setting high standards you are, in effect, saying to each student, "You have the potential to achieve great things." If you expect little, you will certainly achieve it, but if you expect all students to do their best and make significant progress, you will build their competence and confidence. By clearly delineating high expectations and providing all students with the tools to meet them, students will be more likely to make dramatic progress. Of course, you can set unreasonable standards that will hinder learning, but if you know the starting achievement levels for your students, you can then tailor your standards and expectations to stretch their capabilities. Establishing this starting point comes from taking the time to assess each student.

In the article "Music Teaching and Assessment," Richard and Robin Fiese state,

> Assessment is not a goal; it is simply a tool. It is the tool by which we make determinations regarding the musical behaviors of our students. In a very broad sense, the job of a music teacher is to monitor and elicit change regarding the musical behaviors of our students. Since the decisions that we make regarding our students are important (sometimes life-altering), we need to have information that is accurate, relevant, and relatively comprehensive. If you believe that what you teach is important and how you teach is important, then what and how you assess what you teach is no less important because it is all one process.[2]

To start this process, realize that your students will come to you at different stages of achievement development. Your job is to find out where they are (point A) so you can take them as far as possible (point B).

To find out their current level of achievement (point A), use the following steps:

1. Consult the building and district syllabus, if available.
2. Review the National Content Standards for Music Education provided by MENC: The National Association for Music Education, and your state standards of learning, if such standards exist.

3. Review the MENC Performance Standards that provide sequenced benchmarks of progress throughout the grade levels. These standards also contain sample assessments and examples of student responses preK–12 at the basic, proficient, and advanced levels of achievement.
4. Speak with veteran teachers in your building or district to find out the front-line expectations for each grade level (classroom and performance ensembles). These personal expectations will help you understand how the implemented curriculum aligns with the written curriculum and standards of the building, district, and state. Sometimes the written curriculum needs clarification relative to what is actually taught day to day in the classroom.
5. Give a brief written or performance quiz based on what you have discovered by taking steps 1–4.

These steps will help in choosing appropriate levels of literature, materials, and activities to start off the year. As the year goes on you will very likely have to adjust your teaching approaches and support materials because students may not develop according to your plan. To determine student progress over the course of each marking period, academic year, and beyond, develop assessment guides such as sample lesson plan 1, provided in chapter 3. These guides can create a useful picture of each student. At all times make sure that students, parents, and the administration know what you are basing your grades on, how you are determining the grades, how parents can help, and what students can do to achieve success in your class. Assess students early and often to provide useful feedback for yourself, students, and parents. If you assess early on in the year, the students will know where they stand and will have time to improve. These assessments will also give you the opportunity to evaluate your effectiveness and, if needed, modify content and your teaching approaches.

Once you begin the process of documenting student achievement levels and progress, you and your colleagues will benefit from establishing a tracking system that provides information for each student as they move from grade to grade or from building to building. This process will help unify the K–12 program and will be useful in providing information for new teachers, for teachers within your building if a student changes classes or ensembles, for teachers at the same grade level in other buildings, for teachers at other grade levels in other buildings, and for programs in other districts if the student moves. Such systems exist for purchase but you could create your own student tracking file (STF).

This file should contain names of schools attended and teachers; complete contact information; parent or guardian names; achievement level progress documented by year-to-year assessment guides that are linked to state and national standards; and any experiences in Orff, Kodaly, Dalcroze, Gordon, or Suzuki methodologies. The STF should also note participation in large and small performing ensembles (curricular and cocurricular); voice type (including all changes); major instrument; minor instrument; record of private study; solo and chamber literature studied and performed; ensemble literature performed with levels of difficulty; solo and ensemble competition results; all-district, all-county, and all-state rankings and participation; and any other honors and awards. By tracking students in this way, you will be able to plan short and long sequences of instruction without having to construct an achievement background from scratch.

Dedication

- To the success of all types of students
- To excellence and academic rigor
- To your own professional growth

As you read in chapter 4, data collected over the years on outstanding teachers from the Teach for America program show that, among other traits, these teachers "worked relentlessly, refusing to surrender to the combined menaces of poverty, bureaucracy, and budgetary shortfall."[3] Such teachers are dedicated to doing whatever it takes to make sure all students realize their full potential. They are willing to put in long hours of study and preparation, they will never give up on a student, and they will not use any outside factors as a reason for abandoning their hopes for student progress and ultimate success. Will you let deteriorating facilities and equipment, lack of supplies and administrative support, fractured family units, or disinterested fellow teachers deter you from your goals? Are you willing to persevere in the pursuit of excellence?

Dedication involves commitment to excellence and maintaining academic rigor no matter the barriers to learning you face. There are many examples of this type of dedication. Isn't it interesting that wherever certain teachers go, great things just happen to occur? There are music programs that lack funds and facilities but produce quality learning and performances. These positive results happen because of teacher dedication driven by all of the other attributes of attitude we have reviewed. But dedication doesn't stop here.

How dedicated are you to developing your own professional growth? In addition to maintaining your performance skills, it is vital that you seek professional growth and keep up to date on the best instructional practices, education research, and issues that can help or hinder learning. Become involved in professional societies such as MENC, state music educator associations, and organizations that are specific to your area, such as the American String Teachers Association, National Association of Teachers of Singing, the American Choral Directors Association, the Society for General Music, the National Band Association, or the Percussive Arts Society. Review the journals from these organizations and attend their conferences, clinics, and workshops. In addition, network with your professional colleagues to get ideas for teaching approaches, management strategies, new performance literature, and materials.

Structure

- Consistency
- Planning and preparation
- Organization and management (people and paper)

Students seek structure and thrive within it. Don't be afraid of maintaining a consistent opening and ending routine for your classroom or rehearsal. You can vary the content of the routine, but establishing a clear-cut, content-linked structure at the beginning and the ending of each class or rehearsal will help students get focused immediately, provide students with clear expectations, and an encouraging, purposeful learning atmosphere. By using such routines you will gain confidence in implementing the lesson because the class has gotten off to a smooth start.

You increase the likelihood of marked student progress if you work to develop your organizational skills, and your ability to design a sequence of concise, clear lesson plans. Effective teaching is propelled by careful and thorough planning that employs a variety of activities to help students in learning concepts and skills.

In addition, you will be faced with administrative demands that require the production of a mountain of paperwork connected with record keeping, lesson planning, and reports. To be effective in applying what you know to a widely varied student population really requires you to be an administrator and teacher all in one.

It is not too soon to develop finely honed organizational skills and structure. Think about how you function now as a student, at your part-time job, and with your day-to-day personal responsibilities, and determine to have the essential component of structure permeate all that you do.

Character

- Trust and respect
- Reasonableness and fairness

- Ethics and values
- Honor and integrity
- Walking your talk

Some would place the component of character first in a priority listing of important teaching characteristics, because without an underlying sense of the dignity and worth of each student, the other components are houses built on sand foundations. However, it is not always easy to view all students as worthy of your respect. There are attitudes and behaviors exhibited by some students that will make it difficult for you to maintain your dignity. Some of your students will know exactly what buttons to push to cause other students and you to react inappropriately. So it is critically important that you do all you can to create a culture of character in your classroom or rehearsal space. Students will quickly learn that when they enter your classroom or rehearsal area, your expectations will always be based on maintaining a high level of respect. The most powerful way to create this culture of character and classroom atmosphere is to model the behavior you expect from your students. If you speak well, avoid sarcasm and slang, demonstrate self-control and patience, and show that you respect your students, they will tend to respond in kind.

If you are fair, reasonable, and consistent in all of your interactions with students, you will soon notice a natural, mutual respect between you and your students that will be effective in management issues and the overall learning process. This respect will act as a powerful part of a positive learning atmosphere that will help students succeed. By always being honest and honorable, and if you "walk your talk," you can develop a foundation of trust that is essential for leadership and learning.

Summary

In thinking about your future involvement with this noble profession, ask yourself if you are "checked in." To what degree are you committed to the pursuit of excellence? How willing are you to persevere in helping each student become all he or she is capable of becoming? How involved will you become in connecting positively with the constituent network that surrounds and influences each student—family, community, culture, society? How dedicated are you to growing professionally in the six components of effective teaching—content, communication, comprehension, structure, dedication, and character? How involved will you be in developing the growth of students from all subject areas?

In considering the question "Who should be at the wheel of music education?" we can assuredly say that teachers who are committed to developing their effectiveness in interacting with students of all backgrounds and abilities should be the ones who are driving music education in this increasingly complex world. To do otherwise would invite the media, the market, and other external, competing forces to take the wheel. Unless you are content to allow our profession to ride in the back seat, you must become an expert driver of effectiveness. Only then will you and your students be able to enjoy a journey of artistic adventure and joy, and arrive at a meaningful destination of depth, discernment, and fulfillment.[4]

Students' Final Comments

It is appropriate to let students have the last word about the effects of this great art of music we teach. Read and reflect on some additional thoughts of the eighth-grade chorus students we met earlier. These are the students you will be teaching.

> "Music is amazing. It can free you from yourself. It affects our feeling, emotions, and our life. Music is our strongest memory, our strongest hope. It outshines everything in our life, yet is so casual in this time. Making music is amazing—pulling a bow across a string or pushing down a key on a piano and hearing the sound ring out, letting the sound overcome you. It brings out the strongest feelings in all of us as the world's most natural wonder. Even the shape of your lips and a single breath can change your life as the sound envelops you and recreates you without even anyone noticing, even yourself sometimes. Music is the most amazing thing!"

> "Music is wonderful and majestic. I think music speaks louder than words, and what words cannot explain, music is there to save the day."

> "Music is extraordinary. It's beautiful and wonderful. I don't know how anyone goes on without music. When I'm doing my homework I listen to music. It helps me focus. Without music, how can we sing? How can we dance? Music is like a part of my soul. Music is life. If someone didn't know music, I think of the difference it would make if that person knew music. Music is how we praise God. The world would be destroyed without music. It makes people happy and puts a smile on my face when I get to sing a song. That's what music is."

> "Music is my life. It helps me through my day. It's never failed me before and it surely won't today. It's a special language people understand, and

over the years it's been passed down hand-to-hand through all states and foreign lands. It is something that touches me in different ways each time. You could trade me nothing in place of it, not even a gazillion dimes. It helps me enjoy many good times and gets me through the bad. Oh music, sweet music, if I didn't have you, I'd be sad. I don't know about other people, but I do know about me. Music is and always will be my cup of tea."

For Reflection, Discussion, Assignment

1. Choose, or be assigned, one of the six components of effective teaching, and present orally an overview of one resource that relates to that component. Be prepared to discuss how you plan to use what you have learned from the source in your teaching. You may choose a source from the following resources, or use an article or book from any source approved by your instructor.
2. Using the six components of effective teaching, conduct one interview with a preservice music teacher and one interview with an in-service music teacher to learn what others in the profession think about what is important in the teaching and learning process, and how they are seeking professional growth. Remember that the interviews must be completely voluntary and anonymous. It should be more informative if class members interview a mix of student teachers, new teachers (first three years of service), and veterans (more than three years of teaching). Present an oral synopsis of the results of your interviews.
3. Complete the following exercise.

Six Components of Effective Teaching: A Self-Evaluation

Content, communication, comprehension, dedication, structure, and character should form the core of your teaching. To aid in your development in these components complete this self evaluation. After rating yourself in each of the six components of effective teaching, be prepared to discuss how you intend to seek growth in each one. Support your growth plan with specific resources chosen from the following resources or from other sources.

As a result of this exercise you should be able to focus on areas in need of improvement and act to address them. As you evaluate yourself in each of the six components of effective teaching, imagine that you are leading your students through six doors to learning that you will unlock for them by means of your attributes of attitude.

Rate yourself in each of the six components:

1 = poor, 2 = fair, 3 = good, 4 = excellent, 5 = superior

Under each of the six components, note one way you intend to grow professionally in the component and how you will accomplish that growth.

---

1. Content

Mastering subject and technical skills   1 2 3 4 5

Knowing high-quality literature and materials   1 2 3 4 5

Note one way you intend to grow in the area of content and how you will accomplish that growth: _____

2. Communication

Exhibiting cooperation and understanding   1 2 3 4 5

Displaying a natural sense of humor   1 2 3 4 5

Knowing ways to create a positive learning atmosphere   1 2 3 4 5

Knowing how to lead students to learn how to learn   1 2 3 4 5

Involving all students in gaining ownership of what they are studying   1 2 3 4 5

Addressing student needs by knowing a variety of teaching strategies   1 2 3 4 5

Connecting with all components of the students' constituent network   1 2 3 4 5

Note one way you intend to grow in the area of communication and how you will accomplish that growth: _____

3. Comprehension

Setting high standards and giving students the tools to meet or surpass them   1 2 3 4 5

Knowing how to measure student achievement accurately and usefully   1 2 3 4 5

Using student outcomes to measure your teaching effectiveness   1 2 3 4 5

Note one way you intend to grow in the area of comprehension and how you will accomplish that growth: _____

4. **Dedication**

   To the success of all types of students   1 2 3 4 5

   To excellence and academic rigor   1 2 3 4 5

   To your own professional growth   1 2 3 4 5

   Note one way you intend to grow in the area of dedication and how you will accomplish that growth: _____

5. **Structure**

   In your daily life and in your college coursework how do you measure up in the following areas?

   Consistency   1 2 3 4 5

   Planning and preparation   1 2 3 4 5

   Organization and management (people and paper)   1 2 3 4 5

   Note one way you intend to grow in the area of structure and how you will accomplish that growth: _____

6. **Character**

   In your interaction with all people, how do you rate yourself in the following?

   Reasonableness and fairness   1 2 3 4 5

   Trust and respect   1 2 3 4 5

   Ethics and values   1 2 3 4 5

   Honor and integrity   1 2 3 4 5

   Walking your talk   1 2 3 4 5

   Note one way you intend to grow in the area of character and how you will accomplish that growth: _____

Resources

Content

Anderson, William M., and Joy E. Lawrence. *Integrating Music into the Elementary Classroom*, 6th ed. Belmont, CA: Wadsworth Group/Thomson Learning, 2004.

Apfelstadt, Hilary. "First Things First: Selecting Repertoire." *Music Educators Journal* 87, no. 1 (July 2000): 19–22, 46.

Brinson, Barbara A. *Choral Music Methods and Materials: Developing Successful Choral Programs.* New York: Schirmer, 1996.

Campbell, Patricia Shehan, and Carol Scott Kassner. *Music in Childhood*, 3rd ed. New York: Schirmer, 2009.

Cooper, Lynn G. *Teaching Band and Orchestra: Methods and Materials*. Chicago: GIA, 2004.

Edwards, Linda Carol, Kathleen M. Bayless, and Marjorie E. Ramsey. *Music: A Way of Life for the Young Child*, 5th ed. Upper Saddle River, NJ: Pearson Education, 2005.

Hackett, Patricia, and Carolynn A. Lindman. *The Music Classroom: Backgrounds, Models, and Skills for Elementary Teaching*, 8th ed. Upper Saddle River, NJ: Prentice Hall, 2010.

Hallahan, Daniel P., James M. Kauffman, and Paige C. Pullen. *Exceptional Learners: Introduction to Special Education with Cases for Reflection and Analysis and My Education Lab*, 11th ed. Boston: Allyn & Bacon, 2008.

Herrold, Rebecca. *New Approaches to Elementary Classroom Music*, 2nd ed. Upper Saddle River, NJ: Prentice-Hall, 1991.

Persellin, Diane. "The Importance of High-Quality Literature." *Music Educators Journal* 87, no. 1 (July 2000): 17–18.

Rosene, Paul E. "10 Tips for Discovering High-Quality Music for Your Band or Orchestra." *Teaching Music* 11, no. 5 (April 2004): 34.

Spaeth, Jeanne. "Finding Quality Literature for Young Children." *Teaching Music* 2, no. 1 (August 1994): 40–41.

Communication

Bancroft, Tony. *Growing Your Musician: A Practical Guide for Band and Orchestra Parents*. Lanham, MD: Rowman & Littlefield, 2004.

Battisti, Frank L. "Teaching Music: The Leadership Component." *Music Educators Journal* 85, no. 6 (May 1999): 38–40.

Berk, Ronald A. *Humor as an Instructional Defibrillator: Evidence-Based Techniques in Teaching and Assessment*. Sterling, VA: Stylus, 2002.

Bobetsky, Victor V. "Turn Parents into Partners." *Teaching Music* 11, no. 1 (August 2003): 38–41.

Circle, David. "A Vision—Community." *Teaching Music* 12, no. 2 (October 2004): 5.

Marowitz, David R. "Why Your Music Program Needs a Web Site." *Teaching Music* 14, no. 2 (October 2006): 54.

Tamblyn, Doni. *Laugh and Learn*. New York: AMACOM/American Management Association, 2003.

Townsend, Alfred S. "Building Shared Goals in the High School Music Department." *Teaching Music* 14, no. 3 (December 2006): 48–51.

Comprehension

Burrack, Frederick. "Enhanced Assessment in Instrumental Programs." *Music Educators Journal* 88, no. 6 (May 2002): 27–32.

Chiodo, Patricia. "Assessing a Cast of Thousands." *Music Educators Journal* 87, no. 6 (May 2001): 17–23.

Marshall, Herbert D. "Resources for Music Educators: Measuring Achievement in Singing." *General Music Today* 17, no. 2 (Winter 2004): 52.

MENC: The National Association for Music Education. *Spotlight on Assessment in Music Education*. Reston, VA: MENC, 2001.

Rusell, Joshua A., and James R. Austin. "Assessment Practices of Secondary Music Teachers." *Journal of Research in Music Education* 58, no. 1 (April 2010): 37–54.

Scott, Sheila. "Evaluating Tasks for Performance-Based Assessments: Advice for Music Teachers." *General Music Today* 17, no. 2 (Winter 2004): 17.

Dedication and Structure

Maranzo, Robert J., Jana S. Maranzo, and Debra J. Pickering. *Classroom Management That Works: Research-Based Strategies for Every Teacher*. Alexandria, VA: Association for Supervision & Curriculum Development, 2003.

Rush, Scott. *Habits of a Highly Successful Band Director*. Chicago: GIA, 2006.

Townsend, Alfred S. "Common Missteps of New Band and Orchestra Directors." *The Instrumentalist* 64, no. 2 (September 2009): 28–30, 56.

———. "Stop! Look! Listen! for Effective Band Rehearsals." *Teaching Music* 10, no. 4 (February 2003): 23–25.

Character

Abrahams, Frank, and Paul D. Head. *Case Studies in Music Education*, 2nd ed. Chicago: GIA, 2005.

Clark, Ron. *The Essential 55: An Award-Winning Educator's Rules for Discovering the Successful Student in Every Child*. New York: Hyperion, 2004.

Jordan, James. *The Musician's Walk: An Ethical Labyrinth*. Chicago: GIA, 2006.

Lautzenheiser, Tim. *Everyday Wisdom for Inspired Teaching*. Chicago: GIA, 2005.

Lickona, Thomas. *Educating for Character: How Our Schools Can Teach Respect and Responsibility*. New York: Bantam Books, 1991.

MENC: The National Association for Music Education. *Music Makes a Difference: Progress and Partnerships*. Reston, VA: MENC, 1999.

Roth, John, K., ed. *Inspiring Teaching: Carnegie Professors of the Year Speak*. Bolton, MA: Anker, 1997.

Wis, Ramona M. "The Conductor as Servant-Leader." *Music Educators Journal* 89, no. 2 (July 2001): 17–23.

Notes

Chapter 1: The Historical and Research Context of Effective Music Teaching

1. Michael Mark and Charles L. Gary, *A History of American Music Education* (Lanham, MD: Rowman & Littlefield Education, 2007), 127.

2. Ibid., 134.

3. Lois Chosky et al., *Teaching Music in the Twentieth Century*, 2nd ed. (Upper Saddle River, NJ: Prentice-Hall, 2001), 5.

4. Mark and Gary, *American Music Education*, 127.

5. Ibid.

6. Chosky et al., *Teaching Music*, 7.

7. Mark and Gary, *American Music Education*, 163.

8. Ibid., 164.

9. Robert A. Choate, Charles B. Fowler, Charles E. Brown, and Louis G. Wersen, "The Tanglewood Symposium: Music in American Society," *Music Educators Journal* 54, no. 3 (1967): 51.

10. From *National Standards for Arts Education*. Copyright © 1994 by Music Educators National Conference (MENC). Used by permission. The complete National Arts Standards and additional materials relating to the standards are available from MENC: The National Association for Music Education, 1806 Robert Fulton Drive, Reston, VA 20191; www.menc.org.

11. Ibid.

12. H. E. Kratz, "Characteristics of the Best Teacher as Recognized by Children," *Pedagogical Seminary*, no. 3 (June 1896): 413–18.

13. Joe W. Grant and Lynn E. Drafall, "Teacher Effectiveness Research: A Review and Comparison," *Bulletin of the Council for Research in Music Education* 108 (Spring 1991): 31–48.

14. Ibid., 38.

15. Ibid., 39.

16. David J. Teachout, "Preservice and Experienced Teachers' Opinions of Skills and Behaviors Important to Successful Music Teaching," *Journal of Research in Music Education* 45 (Spring 1997): 41–50.

17. Ibid., 45.

18. Ibid.

19. Charles R. Hoffer, *Teaching Music in the Secondary Schools*, 5th ed. (Belmont, CA: Wadsworth/Thomson Learning, 2001), 221–22.

20. Steven N. Kelly, "High School Instrumental Students' Perceptions of Effective Music Student Teacher Traits," *Journal of Music Teacher Education* 17 (Spring 2008): 83–91.

21. Ibid., 83.

22. Ibid., 86.

23. Ibid., 89.

24. Manny Brand, "Music Teacher Effectiveness: Selected Historical and Contemporary Research Approaches," *Australian Journal of Music Education* 1 (2009): 13–18.

25. Ibid., 15.

26. Manny Brand, *The Teaching of Music in Nine Asian Nations: Comparing Approaches to Music Education* (New York: Edwin Mellen Press, 2006).

27. Brand, "Music Teacher Effectiveness," 16.

28. Ibid.

29. Ibid.

30. Peter Miksza, Matthew Roeder, and Dana Biggs, "Surveying Colorado Band Directors' Opinions of Skills and Characteristics Important to Successful Music Teaching," *Journal of Research in Music Education* 57, no. 4 (January, 2010): 364–81.

31. Ibid., 377.

Chapter 2: Artistry in Effective Teaching: Command of Content and Mastery of Methods

1. Alfred S. Townsend, "Driving Music Education: Who's at the Wheel?" *Teaching Music* 16, no. 1 (August 2008): 30.

2. Diane Persellin, "The Importance of High-Quality Literature," *Teaching Music* 87, no. 1 (July 2000): 16.

Chapter 3: Effective Instruction

1. George Katona, *Organizing and Memorizing* (New York: Columbia University Press, 1940), 260.

2. Connie L. Hale and Susan K. Green, "Six Key Principles for Music Assessment," *Music Educators Journal* 95, no. 4 (2009): 27.

3. Ibid., 27–28.

4. Brandi Simonsen et al., "Evidence-based Practices in Classroom Management: Considerations for Research to Practice," *Education and Treatment of Children* 31, no. 3 (2008): 351.

5. William I. Bauer, "Classroom Management for Ensembles," *Music Educators Journal* 14, no. 6 (May 2001): 27.

6. Harry K. Wong and Rosemary T. Wong, *The First Days of School* (Mountain View, CA: Harry K. Wong, 1998), 145.

7. Ibid., 170.

8. Ibid., 171.

9. Debra G. Gordon, "Classroom Management Problems and Solutions," *Music Educators Journal* 88, no. 2 (September 2001): 23.

10. Mary S. Adamek, "Meeting Special Needs in Music Class," *Music Educators Journal* 87, no. 4 (January 2001): 24.

11. Greg Conderman, Sarah Johnston-Rodriquez, Paula Hartman, and Drew Kemp, "What Teachers Should Say and How They Should Say It," *Kappa Delta Pi Record* 46, no. 4 (Summer 2010): 176.

12. Adamek, "Special Needs," 24.

13. Ibid., 25.

14. Ibid., 26.

15. Stephen F. Zdzinski, "Instrumental Music for Special Learners," *Music Educators Journal* 87, no. 4 (January 2001): 29.

16. Ibid.

Chapter 4: The Critical Element: Teacher Attitude

1. Voltaire quote taken from *Quotations On: Moods*, www.cafe-philosophy.com/?q=quotes/moods.

2. Amanda Ripley, "What Makes a Great Teacher?" *The Atlantic Online* (January/February 2010): 4, www.theatlantic.com/doc/201001/good-teaching.

3. Ibid., 5.

4. Ibid., 8.

5. *Webster's New World Dictionary of the American Language*, 2nd ed., s.v. "xerophilous."

6. Haim G. Ginott, *Teacher and Child: A Book for Parents and Teachers* (New York: Macmillan, 1972), 13.

Chapter 5: Effective Communication and Six Components of Effective Teaching: Artistry and Attitude Together

1. Alfred S. Townsend, "Building Shared Goals in the High School Music Department," *Teaching Music* 14, no. 3 (December 2006): 51.

2. Sharyn L. Battersby, "Increasing Awareness in the General Music Classroom," *General Music Today* 22, no. 3 (Spring 2009): 1.

3. William J. Seiller and Melissa L. Beall, *Communication: Making Connections*, 7th ed. (New York: Pearson Education, 2008), 111.

4. Ibid., 110.

5. Ibid., 130.

6. Alfred S. Townsend, "Implement a 'Connecting Parents with Learning Project' in Your School," *Music Educators Journal* 97, no. 1 (September 2010): 45–48. Copyright 2010 MENC: The National Association for Music Education (DOI: 10.1177/0027432109332736), http://mej.sagepub.com.

7. U.S. Department of Education, "Engaging Parents in Education: Lessons from Five Parental Information and Resource Centers," 2007, www.ed.gov/admins/comm/parents/parentinvolve/engagingparents.pdf, 2.

8. Diana Hiatt-Michael, "Preparing Teachers to Work with Parents," Washington, DC: ERIC Clearinghouse on Teaching and Teacher Education, 2001, 1, www.ericdigests.org/2002-3/parents.html.

9. Townsend, "Implement a 'Connecting Parents with Learning Project,'" 48.

10. William J. Seiller and Melissa L. Beall, *Communication: Making Connections*, 7th ed. (New York: Pearson Education, 2008), 5. Source: National Association of Colleges & Employers, *Job Outlook 2003*; 21st Century Workforce Commission, *A Nation of Opportunity: Strategies for Building Tomorrow's 21st Century Workforce* (Washington, DC: U.S. Department of Labor, 2003).

Chapter 6: Effective Leadership

1. John C. Maxwell, *The 21 Irrefutable Laws of Leadership*, 10th ed. (Nashville, TN: Thomas Nelson, 2007), 146.

2. Ibid., 51.

3. Terry Pearce, "Leadership Coaching . . . A Contact Sport," *San Francisco Examiner*, April 30, 2000, www.terrypearce.com/tp-art-coaching.html.

4. Maxwell, *21 Irrefutable Laws of Leadership*, 64.

5. Ibid., 65.

6. Ibid., 61.

7. Ramona M. Wis, "The Conductor as Servant-Leader," *Music Educators Journal* 89, no. 2 (July 2002): 22.

8. James M. Kouzes and Barry Z. Posner, *The Truth about Leadership* (San Francisco, CA: Jossey-Bass, 2010), 7. James M. Kouzes is the dean's executive professor of leadership, Leavey School of Business at Santa Clara University. Barry Z. Posner is professor of leadership at Santa Clara University.

9. Ibid., 19–20.

10. Nancy K. Klein, Ph.D., has won several awards from Old Dominion University that reflect her effectiveness as a teacher-leader. Selected awards include the Robert L. Stern Award for Excellence in Teaching, College of Arts and Letters; the Shining Star Award for commitment to student growth and development; the Joel S. Lewis Award for Excellence in Student Mentoring, College of Arts and Letters; and the Most Inspiring Faculty Award (twice). Klein has been invited to conduct select honors choirs regionally and for international concert tours. In addition, she presents numerous leadership workshops and papers at national and international conferences. Nancy K. Klein, associate professor of music, interview with the author, September 2010.

11. James J. Cassara has served as an exemplary education leader in several capacities. He was an arts administrator in two large Long Island, New York, public school districts and was elected president of the New York State School Music Association, the Suffolk County Music Educators Association, and the New York State Council of Administrators of Music Education. Cassara is active as a performer, holding the solo alto saxophone chairs in the Atlantic Wind Symphony and the American Concert Band, both on Long Island, New York. James J. Cassara, adjunct professor of music education, Long Island University, e-mail responses to author's questions, September 28, 2010.

12. Steven E. Schopp, Ed.D., has distinguished himself as a music education leader and teacher. He has received many honors including distinguished service awards from the New York Metropolitan Youth Orchestra, the New York State Council of Administrators of Music Education, and the New York State School Music Association. He also received the Leadership Award from the New York City Black Music Caucus. Steven E. Schopp, executive director, New York State School Music Association, e-mail responses to author's questions, September 18, 2010.

13. John W. Gardner, *On Leadership* (New York: Free Press, 1990), 199.

Chapter 7: Forming Your Personal Philosophy of Music Education: What Do You Believe Is Important in Teaching and Learning Music?

1. Linda K. Thompson, "Considering Beliefs in Learning to Teach Music," *Music Educators Journal* 93 (January 2007): 30.

2. Lynn G. Cooper, *Teaching Band and Orchestra: Methods and Materials* (Chicago: GIA, 2004), 358.

3. *The Dialogues of Plato*, 3rd ed., trans. B. Jowett (Oxford: Clarendon Press, 1892), 2: 47.

Chapter 8: Case Studies: Artistry and Attitude in Action

1. John Corigliano, taped telephone interview with the author, October 1983 in "Unity and Variety in 'A Dylan Thomas Trilogy' by John Corigliano (1938–)" (Alfred S. Townsend, Ph.D. dissertation, New York University, 1986), 10, 11.

2. Ashley Phillips is in her second year of teaching music in two inner-city schools. She earned baccalaureate and master degrees in music education from Hampton University, Hampton, Virginia. Honors and awards include Alpha Kappa Mu honor society, Golden Key honor society, and the National Dean's List. Telephone conversation and e-mail responses to author's questions, September 25, 2010.

3. Frank Garcia has taught band and orchestra in southeastern Virginia high schools and is active as a performer. Garcia has held many local and state leadership positions in professional music educator organizations. He has won awards for outstanding teaching and service. Selected awards include the ALLI Award from the Cultural Alliance of Greater Hampton Roads, Virginia, for distinguished contributions to the arts; Teacher of the Year Salem High School; Claus Noble Educator of Distinction; Virginia Beach City Public Schools Distinguished Educator (three times); PTSA Award for distinguished service (multiple schools).

4. Frank Garcia is chairman of the Visual and Performing Arts Academy and the Salem High School Fine Arts Department, and director of instrumental music, orchestra director, and lead mentor for all students in all subjects at Salem High School, Virginia Beach, Virginia. Interview with the author, August 2010.

5. Ernest L. Boyer, *Scholarship Reconsidered: Priorities of the Professoriate* (San Francisco, CA: Jossey-Bass, 1990), 24.

Chapter 9: Administering Your Program

1. From the MENC.org website, *The United States Copyright Law: A Guide for Music Educators*, www.menc.org/resources/view/united-states-copyright-law-a-guide-for-music-educators-part-1#intro.

Chapter 10: Summary

1. Alfred S. Townsend, "Driving Music Education: Who's at the Wheel?" *Teaching Music* 16, no. 1 (August 2008): 30.

2. Richard K. Fiese and Robin E. Fiese, "Music Teaching and Assessment," *Spotlight on Assessment in Music Education* (Reston, VA: MENC: The National Association for Music Education, 2001), 13.

3. Amanda Ripley, "What Makes a Great Teacher?" *The Atlantic Online* (January/February 2010): 4, www.theatlantic.com/doc/201001/good-teaching.

4. Townsend, "Driving Music Education," 32.

Index

About the Author

Alfred S. Townsend is an associate professor of music at Old Dominion University, Norfolk, Virginia, where he holds the F. Ludwig Diehn Chair in Instrumental Music Education, and teaches undergraduate and graduate courses in music education and research. His articles have appeared in the *Music Educators Journal*, *Teaching Music*, *Choral Journal*, *National Band Association Journal*, the *Instrumentalist*, and *Il Saggiatore Musicale* (University of Bologna). Over the course of many years he has served as a public school district music administrator and teacher, university professor, and ensemble director.